READING GAMES

A Collection of Reading Games and Activities for intermediate to Advanced Students of English

Jill and Charles Hadfield

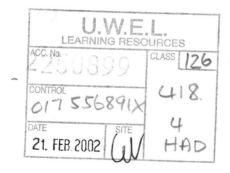

 LONGMAN

Pearson Education Limited
Edinburgh Gate, Harlow,
Essex CM20 2JE, England

© Jill Hadfield and Charles Hadfield, 1995
The moral right of the Author to be identified has been asserted.

Designed by Tony Richardson

This edition published by Addison Wesley Longman Ltd 1996.
Fifth impression 1999

ISBN 0-17-556891-X

Printed in China
NPCC/05

Acknowledgements

The authors are very grateful to the staff and students of South Devon College for inspiring, trying out and commenting on these materials and to Sally McGugan and Maria Stebbing for their skilful, patient and good-humoured editing.

Texts

The publishers are grateful to the following for permission to reproduce copyright material. They have tried to contact all copyright holders, but in cases where they may have failed will be pleased to make the necessary arrangements at the first opportunity.

Rodgers, Coleridge and White for extracts from *The Book of Heroic Failures* by Stephen Pile (Game 3).
Bloomsbury Publishing Ltd for extracts from *No Time to Wave Goodbye* by Ben Wicks published by Bloomsbury Publishing Ltd, 1989 (Game 7).
Virgin Publishing Ltd for extracts from *The Return of Urban Myths* by Phil Healey and Rick Glanvill published by Virgin Publishing Ltd (Game 8).
BAA Communications for their advertisement 'Watch Your Body Language' (Game 10).
The author for extracts from *Ordinary Lives* by Carol Adams (Game 11).
Oxford University Press for extracts © Iona and Peter Opie 1959. Reprinted from *The Lore and Language of Schoolchildren* by Iona and Peter Opie (1959) by permission of Oxford University Press (Game 12).
Sunday Times Syndication for extracts from 'A Life in the Day' articles in *The Sunday Times Colour Supplement* (Game 14).
Oxford University Press for 'The Frog Maiden' from *Burmese Folk Tales* by Martin Htin Aung (Game 21).
Routledge and Kegan Paul for 'Beauty and Pockface' from *Chinese Fairy Tales and Folk Tales* by Wolfram Eberhard (Game 21).
Foulsham and Co. Ltd for extracts from *Old Moore's Dream Almanack* (Game 23).
Harper Collins Publishers Ltd for extracts from *The Politically Correct Dictionary* by H. Beard and C. Cerf (Game 24).

Photographs

The publishers are grateful to the following for permission to reproduce photographs:

Stuart Boreham Photography, The Hulton Picture Company.
The Hutchison Library, Nelson ELT, Rex Features Limited.
The Sunday Times/Marie-Sara Bourseiller/Maya Angelou/Rosemary Henderson.

Illustrations
Phill Burrows (Game 24)

Contents

	List of games	Level	Function
1	Parlour games	intermediate	giving instructions
2	Successful failures	intermediate	narrating past events
3	Heroic failures	intermediate	narration
4	Punch lines	intermediate	narration
5	My first valentine	intermediate	narrating past events
6	Postcards from John	intermediate	describing scenes and past events
7	Evacuees	intermediate	narrating past experiences
8	Urban myths	intermediate	narration
9	Famous last words	intermediate	reporting what other people said
10	Body language	upper intermediate	describing customs
11	Time warp	upper intermediate	talking about life in past times
12	Curious customs	upper intermediate	describing habits and customs
13	Village gossip	upper intermediate	narrating past events
14	A life in the day	upper intermediate	describing daily routines
15	Guilty secrets	upper intermediate	narrating past experiences
16	Loose morals	upper intermediate	narrating a story
17	Roots	upper intermediate	talking about past events
18	Ghost stories	upper intermediate	narrating a story
19	Murder in the library	upper intermediate	narration, hypothesis
20	Believe it or not	upper intermediate	defining and explaining, justifying, giving reasons
21	Trouble with men, frogs, shoes and sisters	upper intermediate	narrating a fairy story
22	Horoscope exchange	advanced	talking about character and emotions
23	Dream merchants	advanced	narrating past events, predicting the future
24	Politically correct	advanced	finding euphemisms

For

Laura, Jessica and Rory

The activities in this book all require the reading of a text and the communication of the information it contains, sometimes in order to solve a puzzle or complete a task, sometimes in order to do a role play.

All the activities consist of two main phases:

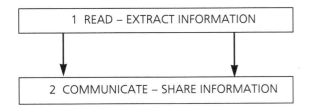

These phases may be organised in different ways. For example, in the first phase, students may be divided into groups and each group given a different text to read. They complete a worksheet and/or discuss the text in their groups.

Phase 1

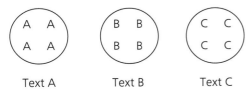

In the second phase students are regrouped to share their information, in order to act out roles or to complete a task or solve a puzzle.

Phase 2

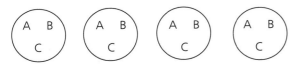

The above diagrams show groupings for an activity involving three texts, but activities may involve from two to six texts.

Alternatively, every student in the class may have a different, short text to read:

Phase 1

A B C D E F G H I J K L M N O P etc.

In phase 2 the students mingle freely and communicate their information in randomly constituted small groups. This activity may have a time limit set by the teacher, and the aim is to listen to as many people's stories as possible (i.e. to obtain as much information as possible) in the time allowed.

Phase 2

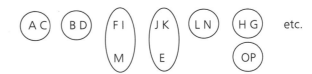

In this type of activity a worksheet or questionnaire is handed out after phase 2 and the students try to complete as much as possible using the information they picked up in the second phase.

Although not an integral part of the 'read and retell' activity, 'lead-in' and 'follow-up' activities have been suggested in most cases to provide further integration of skills. The 'lead-in' activities are based on discussion or listening to an anecdote told by the teacher; the 'follow-up' activities are suggestions for written work.

A list of 'problem vocabulary' – words that may be unfamiliar to the students – is provided in the Teacher's Notes for each game, to enable the teacher to be prepared for queries. Students should be encouraged to read as fluently and self-reliantly as possible, trying to guess or deduce meaning where possible, using English-English dictionaries where this fails, and turning to the teacher for guidance if either of these resources fail.

The Teacher's Notes also give indications of level – the majority of texts are intermediate/upper intermediate level, but where texts are easier or more difficult than average, this is indicated. The time required is also indicated. Most activities will last an average lesson. Shorter activities can be extended to fill a lesson by doing the follow-up activity in class. Longer ones can fill a double lesson, or a single one if the texts is given to the students in advance, or the information 'share phase' allowed to run on into homework.

The activities provide practice both in reading skills and in oral expression, training students in the ability to extract essential information from a text and to give an oral summary of its contents. They provide a stimulus for natural and meaningful communication: giving both a reason and a motivating and enjoyable context for sharing information. When integrating skills in this way, the reading skill feeds directly into the speaking skill: new words and expressions are often absorbed almost effortlessly from the text by a kind of osmosis and students' fluency and confidence in speaking are improved.

Although the activities are quite simple to set up, classroom management needs to be detailed and precise, and you will need to be very clear in your own mind about who is going to do what when – and where! Some points to bear in mind:

● Arrange desks and tables into groups in advance if possible for the first phase. If it is not possible to move the furniture in your classroom, give the same texts to students at adjacent desks, and work out how they can turn their chairs round to talk to those sitting near or behind them, if group discussion is required in the first phase.

• The regrouping of students for the second phase is best done by giving each student a number, e.g.:

Group A	Group B	Group C
1, 2, 3, 4	1, 2, 3, 4	1, 2, 3, 4

Then ask 'All the ones' to go to a certain area of the room, 'All the twos' to another area, and so on.

• If students are not in groups, but moving about freely for the second phase, make sure in advance that you have an area where they can do this, by having the desks in a U-shape with the central area free, or if the tables are arranged in groups, by making sure that there is plenty of free space in the central area. If you cannot move your furniture, and your classroom is cramped, you will need to modify this activity, so that students begin by talking to the person next to them, then swap seats with other students to talk to a different partner. The seat-swapping had probably better be directed by you if space is limited!

• The teacher's role changes constantly during one of these activities, and you will need to be quite a chameleon. During the initial setting-up phase, and the changeover from phase 1 to phase 2, you will need to be a very clear instruction-giver. During phase 1, your role will be that of guide and problem-solver. You may need to be very quick on your feet here if you have a large class. If the students are working in groups, try to train them to ask each other for help first before turning to you – they can often solve each others' problems. During phase 2, your role is as a resource and guide, helping students if they are stuck and don't know what to say, or are unclear about what to do. You are also a monitor and evaluator, listening to what the students are saying and noting mistakes and areas of difficulty, which may form a basis for subsequent teaching. It is a good idea to carry a pen and notebook, or an OHT and OHP pen if you have one, and to note down any persistent problems or errors.

• The longer texts have an accompanying worksheet to direct the students' attention to the main points and to help them read for gist. With the shorter texts, the instruction is simply to memorise the details. It is important that the students understand that they are not expected to memorise the text and reproduce it word for word, but to understand and remember the main points and retell the story in their own words (though of course they may use words and phrases from the text if they remember them). With stronger groups, or students, it is a good idea to remove the text at the end of phase 1. Weaker students may like to keep the text as a prop, but you should try to ensure that they do not simply read from the text! Ask them to turn it over and only peep at it if they are absolutely desperate, or in the activities which involve retelling the story a few times, let them retain the text at first, and ask them to give it up when they have told the story once or twice and are feeling more confident.

• The introductory and follow-up activities are there as suggestions only. You may have your own ideas for introducing or following on from the 'read and retell' activities, but in general some sort of warm-up activity should be included as an introduction, to awaken students' interest and provide a context for the reading text. A follow-up writing task is a valuable activity, partly to 'fix' in more permanent form the new words and expressions the students may have learned during the reading and speaking activities, but also because writing is easier given a context and a reason, and that is precisely what these activities provide.

TEACHER'S NOTES

1 Parlour games

Type of activity
jigsaw in four groups then groups of four
reading instructions and explaining how to play a game

Level/Time required
intermediate/average

Games material
Texts: A Botticelli; B The parson's cat; C Crambo; D The adverb game

Function practised
giving instructions

Structures
imperatives, present simple, must

Lexical areas
famous people, adjectives, adverbs

Problem vocabulary

A Botticelli: *recalled, guess, clues, identity, restrict*

B The parson's cat: *take turns, version, round*

C Crambo: *clue, rhymes, guess*

D The adverb game: *adverb, missing, recalled, guess, perform, according to*

How to use the activity

Make enough copies of text A for one quarter of the students to have a copy each, and the same for texts B, C and D.
The texts in this activity are all instructions for how to play Victorian parlour games, a popular evening pastime in the days before television. Lead into the activity with a brief discussion on what students' families do for entertainment. Divide the class into four groups, A, B, C, and D. Give everyone in group A a copy of text A, everyone in group B a copy of text B, and so on.
Give them time to read their text and discuss any problems or misunderstandings with their group. Tell them that they will have to show other people how to play their game, and warn them that you will take the texts away. They can make notes if they like.
When you are confident they have understood how to play their game, take the texts away and regroup them into fours so that each new group contains an A, a B, a C and a D.
The object of the activity is for each member of the new group to show the rest of the group how to play their game.

Follow-up: Ask students to write a set of instructions for playing a game familiar to them.

2 Successful failures

Type of activity
jigsaw in six groups then groups of six
retelling the history of a successful person and completing a questionnaire

Level/Time required
intermediate/average

Games material
Texts: A Author; B Actress; C Footballer; D Pop singer; E Cartoonist; F Actor
Questionnaire

Function practised
narrating past events

Structures
past tenses

Lexical areas
work, books, acting, football, pop music, art

Problem vocabulary

A A successful author: *dead-end jobs, degree, senior lecturer, ego, took off, paratrooper, kidnap, motivation, put me down, on your side*

B A famous actress: *voluptuous, audition, agent, burst into tears, troupe, modelling, misery, obligations*

C A successful footballer: *trial, rejected, contract, on loan, reluctant, establish, confidence*

D A successful pop singer: *settle down, disbanded, keyboard, tick, on the dole, yell, breakthrough, released, risks*

E A successful cartoonist: *commercial, sold out, desperate, hell on earth, potential, reviewed, genius*

F A successful actor: *cope with, audition, registrar, convinced, encouragement, principal, therapist, evaluate, realised, establishment, scaring, literate, pedlar*

How to use the activity

Make enough copies of text A for one sixth of the students to have a copy each, and the same for texts B-F. Make enough copies of the questionnaire for the students to have one each.
You might like to begin with a short discussion of success and failure. Ask the students to think of and write down the names of one person they think is a success and one person they think is a failure (not necessarily famous people). When they have written down the names, they should get together with a partner and explain why they chose those people and what they mean by success and failure (in whose eyes, by what standards, etc.).
Divide the class into six groups, A, B, C, D, E and F. Give text A to each student in group A, text B to those in group B, etc. Give each student a copy of the questionnaire.
Give them time to read their text, while you circulate to deal with problems and queries.When they have finished reading, ask each student to work with a partner from the same group. Ask one of them to imagine they are the 'successful failure' and the other to imagine they are the person/one of the people who told them some years ago that they wouldn't make it. They meet again at a party and begin to talk...
When the students have finished this first role-play, regroup them so that each new group contains, as far as possible, an A, a B, a C, a D, an E and an F. Ask them to tell their stories to each other.
The object of the activity is to decide who was the biggest failure and who is the biggest success.

Key: Answers to the questionnaire will vary for each character.

Follow-up: Ask students to write the diary entry for their character the day they were told they were no good. Alternatively, pin up a set of pictures of men and women. Ask the students to choose a face that they like. They should then imagine and write a similar failure/success story for that character.

3 Heroic failures

Type of activity
whole class mêlée then groups of four
retelling a story and answering a questionnaire

Level/Time required
intermediate/shorter than average

Games material
Texts: A The crimes that were easiest to detect; B The least well-planned robbery; C The least profitable robbery; D The most unsuccessful prison escape; E The worst bank robbers; F The most unsuccessful attempt to work through a lunch hour; G The least successful attempt to meet a relative at an airport; H The least successful animal rescue; I The least successful bank robber; J The worst tourist
Questionnaire

Function practised
narration

Structures
past tenses

Lexical areas
crime, office work, tourism

Problem vocabulary

A The crimes that were easiest to detect: *dazzling, logic, inevitability, barge, dock strike, craft*

B The least well-planned robbery: *raiding, cash, premises, masks, getaway car, sped, screeched to a halt, omitted*

C *The least profitable robbery: unique, tactic, till, trolley, goods, snatch, undeterred, getaway, raid, scream*

D The most unsuccessful prison escape: *convicts, guided, genius, courtroom, sentenced, judges, jail*

E The worst bank robbers: *stuck, revolving, sheepishly, cashier, practical joke, disheartened, gang, barely, awkwardly, clutching, ankle, getaway, trapped*

F The most unsuccessful attempt to work through a lunch hour: *set a record, uninterrupted, clambered, adjoining, stared, charged, retreated, steadily, scattered, stacks, heifer, chew, elaborate, pulleys*

G The least successful attempt to meet a relative at an airport: *facilities, wandered, smothered, cuddling, enthusiasm, hospitality, modified, ushered, amiss, slumped, kidnapped*

H The least successful animal rescue: *rescue, strike, valiantly, emergency, retrieve, trapped, haste, discharge, duty, grateful, fond farewell*

I The least successful bank robber: *hold-up, cashier, bemused, grille, fled*

J The worst tourist: *assumed, delayed, heavy traffic, mentioned, tracking down, modernization, brushed aside, landmarks, benefit, tongue, brief, brilliance, siren*

How to use the activity
Make enough copies of the ten texts, A-J, for the students to have one text each, with as much variety as possible in the class. Make enough copies of the questionnaire for the students to have one each.

Explain to the students that they are going to read a story about a disastrous experience. You might like to introduce the activity with an amusing disaster story of your own, or by eliciting tales of personal disaster (funny) from the students. Give out one text to each student and give them some time to read their text, asking you for help if necessary, and to memorise the main points of their story. Then ask them all to stand up and circulate, retelling their story in their own words to as many people as possible.

The object of the activity is to hear as many disaster stories as possible.

You can put a time limit on this part of the activity if you like. After a certain time, ask the students to return to their seats and give them each a copy of the questionnaire. Ask the students to complete as much as possible by themselves, then move them into groups of four and ask them to share their information to complete the questionnaire.

Go through the answers to the questionnaire with the whole class, clearing up any misunderstandings and filling any gaps. Students will probably want to see all the texts.

Note: With a strong group you can remove the texts when they have read them and ask them to tell the stories from memory. With weaker students I often let them keep the texts as support to begin with, then remove them after they have retold the story a couple of times and are feeling more confident.

Key: 1 The prisoners' tunnel came out in the courtroom. 2 There was a dock strike and his was the only boat moving on the water. 3 The Post Office had closed down. 4 There was less in the till than the £10 he had given the cashier. 5 The robbers got stuck in the revolving doors. 6 A cow falling through the roof. 7 She thought a total stranger was her brother. 8 The firemen ran it over. 9 'I don't have a paper bag.' 10 He got off the plane during a fuel stop because he thought he had arrived. New York.

Follow-up: Students could write their own disaster stories, either from experience or imagination. Try giving some titles: The worst charter flight, The worst holiday, The worst piano recital, etc.

4 Punch lines

Type of activity
whole class mêlée
retelling jokes and finding the person with the punch line

Level/Time required
intermediate/shorter than average

Games material
Texts: Jokes 1-15
Punch lines

Function practised
narration

Structures
past tenses

Lexical areas
various

....

Problem vocabulary

1: *vicar, parishioner, parrot, ribbon, hymn, perch*
2: *crumpled, elephant, proves*
3: *penguin*
4: *cautiously, crept*
5: *survey, colonel, achievement*
6: *scrambled*
7: *canary, cuttle fish, wedged, swing, bird seed*
8: *bumped into, bitterly, pregnant, hiccups*
9: *anxious, apologetically*
10: *to the point, romance, royalty, mystery, religion, task, pregnant*
11: *speech, faultless, deafening applause*
12: *achieve, conductor, proposed, free of charge*
13: *weedy, lumberjack, axe blow, crashing*
14: *architect, politician, rib, chaos*
15: *tycoon, flair, specialist, prematurely, worn out, transplant surgery, legal, ridiculous*

....

How to use the activity

Make enough copies of the fifteen jokes for the students to have one joke each, with as much variety as possible in the class. Copy the same number of corresponding punch lines. Give out one joke to each student and one punch line to each student. The punch line should not correspond to the joke the student has! Make sure that somewhere in the class there is a punch line for every joke. If you have more than fifteen students, do the activity in two groups.
Students should read their joke and walk around the class telling it until they find the person who has the corresponding punch line.
The object of the activity is to find their own punch line and to give away their original punch line.
When they have done this, they should sit down. When everyone is sitting down, students can tell their complete jokes to the whole class.

....

Key: The punch lines are printed together on one page in the same order as the jokes appear.

....

Follow-up: Students tell jokes they know – in English!

5 My first valentine

Type of activity
whole class mêlée then pairwork/small groups
retelling an anecdote and completing a questionnaire

Level/Time required
intermediate/shorter than average

Games material
Texts: A Rabbi; B Pin-up/singer; C News presenter; D Sportswoman; E Writer; F Novelist 1; G TV presenter; H Novelist 2; I Politician; J Scriptwriter
Questionnaire

Function practised
narrating past events

Structures
past tenses

Lexical areas
childhood, love

....

Problem vocabulary

A Rabbi: *glamorous, upset, out of reach*
B Pin-up/singer: *promptly, teased, dishy, lipstick, jealous, boasting, annoyed*
C News presenter: *unforgettable, violets, checked, spots*
D Sportswoman: *silk, propose, depressed, ignore, signed*
E Writer: *humiliated, thrilling*
F Novelist 1: *idealistic, garlanded, trimmed,lace*
G TV Presenter: *hideously, cruellest, waded, tadpoles*
H Novelist 2: *puzzled, marvellous, liar*
I Politician: *anonymous, dressing table*
J Scriptwriter: *knock, incredible, do the trick*

....

How to use the activity

Make enough copies of the ten texts, A-J, for the students to have one text each, with as much variety as possible in the class. Make enough copies of the questionnaire for the students to have one each.
You might like to start with a brief introduction of your own about Valentine's Day: explain the history, customs, tell anecdotes, etc. or, if you have a class who are familiar with Valentine's Day, elicit information and/or anecdotes from them.
Give out one text to each student, ensuring that as far as possible everyone gets a different text. If you have twenty or more in your class, it is probably best to do the activity in two groups.
Ask the students to read their text and to memorise the information it contains, in order to be able to tell the story to other students.
While they are reading, circulate and deal with queries.
When they are ready, ask them to get up and walk around the class, telling their story to other students.
The object of the activity is to listen to as many stories as possible in order to complete a questionnaire later.
You might like to give a time limit for this activity. With a strong group, you can collect in the stories. With a weaker group, you may like to let them retain the stories as support

initially but collect them in when they have retold their story once or twice and have more confidence.

When the students have finished or the time limit is up, ask them to sit down and give each student a copy of the questionnaire. Students should try to complete the questionnaire individually, but when they have got as far as they can on their own, they can help each other in pairs or small groups.

Key: 1 A figure with a red heart. 'I'll be loving you'. Yes, he's her husband. 2 Frou-Frou. His secretary. With a lipstick kiss. He opened it. 3 He waded into a pool to get her tadpoles. 4 Two. 5 One. 6 Her first love – a family friend. 7 Seven. A handsome boy. A boy with spots. 8 It asked her to propose to him.

Follow-up: Write your own Valentine anecdote – real or imaginary. Design a Valentine's card.

6 Postcards from John

Type of activity
whole class mêlée then pairwork
retelling news from a postcard and plotting a journey on a map

Level/Time required
intermediate/shorter than average

Games material
Texts: A Delhi; B Kathmandu 1; C Kathmandu 2; D Calcutta; E Mandalay; F Chiang Mai; G Hong Kong; H Bali; I Sydney
Route map

Function practised
describing scenes and past events

Structures
past tenses, present perfect, present simple and continuous

Lexical areas
foreign travel, landscapes, cityscapes, etc.

Problem vocabulary

A Delhi: *immigration, curfew, riots, demonstration, stuck*

B Kathmandu 1: *hellish, wing (of a house), palace, arrested, smuggling, mistaken identity, freed, case, trekking*

C Kathmandu 2: *trekked, temple, yeti, sherpa, scuffling, grabbed, torch, creature, all fours, rucksack, trial*

D Calcutta: *ashamed, perspective, mugged*

E Mandalay: *ruined, temples, crocodile*

F Chiang Mai: *tribe, ethnic, costume, trek, idyllic, kidnapped, bandits, opium smuggling, civil war, guerrillas, jungle, camouflage, armed*

G Hong Kong: *wandering, super, bustle, stopover*

H Bali: *tropical, paradise, cobras, heaven, froze, scream, stroke of luck, pounced, grabbed*

I Sydney: *wheelchair, knocked down, ribs, loan, plaster*

How to use the activity

Make enough copies of the nine postcard texts, A-I, for the students to have one each, with as much variety in the class as possible. Make enough copies of the route map for the students to have one each.

You might like to begin by asking what is the longest journey any of your students have undertaken. Then give everyone a postcard and a route map. If you have fewer than nine students, give some people more than one card. If you have more than nine but fewer than eighteen students, explain that some cards will be duplicates. If you have eighteen or more students, play the game in two groups.

Tell the students that they have all received cards from a mutual friend called John who is travelling in Asia. Ask them to read their card and to plot on the map the section of the journey he describes. They should also mark the map with the appropriate symbol for the adventure that took place in that country. Go round the class and help as required.

When they have finished ask everyone to stand up and move around talking to other people to find out news about John. **The object of the activity is to plot John's journey on the map and mark each country with the appropriate symbol.**

As they finish ask them to sit down with a partner and to compare maps.

Key: Delhi (closed bank); Kathmandu (prison bars); Kathmandu (yeti); Calcutta (passport); Mandalay (crocodile); Chiang Mai (guns); Hong Kong (bath); Bali (snake); Sydney (hospital bed).

Follow-up: Ask students to write one more postcard from John from an interim town in one of the countries he visited. Alternatively, bring in old postcards of your own with blank paper glued to the back. Ask the students to look at the picture, imagine what John did there and write the card.

7 Evacuees

Type of activity
whole class mêlée then pairwork/small groups
retelling an evacuee's experiences and completing extracts from their letters home

Level/Time required
intermediate (though introductory passage is harder)/shorter than average

Games material
Texts: Introductory text; A; B; C; D; E; F; G; H
Worksheet

Function practised
narrating past experiences

Structures
past tenses

Lexical areas
war, domestic life

Problem vocabulary

Introductory text: *urban, threat, rural, idyllic, hell, evacuation, masterpiece, profound, uprooted, gas mask, dispatched, amounted to, cockney, manure, come in for my share of, take someone in, halcyon, city slicker, vulnerable, air raid, inkling, momentous*

A: *pilchards, wallop, dish up*

B: *spots, eventually, nod, bairns*

C: *peacocks, billets, vicar, gear-lever, swastika, bobby, interrogate*

D: *fortunate, viaduct, rails, sigh of relief*

E: *greasy, plait, braid, scullery, consent, allowance, treated*

F: *tortoise, put to sleep, bravely, vet, cargo, forced, sorrowfully*

G: *bolted, crawled, straw, dashing*

H: *devise, insist, unsealed, deposited, accommodated, overjoyed*

How to use the activity

Copy an introductory text and a worksheet for each student. Make enough copies of the eight texts, A-H, for the students to have one each, with as much variety as possible in the class.

Use the introductory text and pictures to stimulate discussion on evacuees: How did the children feel? How did their parents feel as they saw them off at the station? What problems and difficulties would there be for the host families?, etc.

Give out one text describing an evacuee's experience to each student, ensuring that as far as possible everyone gets a different text. If there are more than eight in your class, do the activity in groups.

Ask the students to read the text and assimilate the information, while you circulate and deal with any queries. When they have finished, ask them to stand up and walk around the class, telling their story. They should tell the story as if they were the evacuees and the events happened to them. With a strong group, the texts can be collected in as soon as they have finished reading: weaker students may find it helpful to retain the texts until they have retold their story a couple of times and are feeling more confident.

The object of the activity is to listen to as many stories as possible in order to be able to complete a worksheet.

You can set a time limit for this part of the activity if you like. When they have finished, or the time limit is up, ask them to sit down again and give them a worksheet to complete. They should try to complete this individually as far as possible, but may work in pairs or small groups to help each other when they have done as much as they can by themselves.

Key: 1 a tin of pilchards and some bread and water...for the butter...wallop round the head. 2 we were two plain little girls wearing glasses. 3 him...his son. 4 the train came off the rails and we fell into the water underneath. 5 plait...braid it...5 p.m....money comes from our parents...we get medicine. 6 the vet...soldier...the tortoise...vet...put him in the park. 7 outside...the chicken house...she brought me in...holes   coat. 8 our letters from home and insisted on reading our letters...wrote to tell our parents we were unhappy...the door locked and our belongings in the garden ...seafront...lady with a dog...we could go home with her.

Follow-up: Students can imagine they are one of the evacuees and write a letter home to their parents about their new life.

8   Urban myths

Type of activity
whole class mêlée or groups of eight
retelling a story and finding the person with the ending

Level/Time required
intermediate/average

Games material
Texts: A Take a break; B A nasty set-to; C A low note; D Phone home; E Signed, sealed and delivered; F An unfair cop; G Tow job; H Fitted-up wardrobe
Endings 1-8

Function practised
narration

Structures
past simple, past perfect, past continuous

Lexical areas
crime, driving

Problem vocabulary

A Take a break: *laden down, scruffy, punk, fuming, gathering up, storming out*

B A nasty set-to: *mates, cement mixer truck, thrilled him to bits, soft-top, fist, brim, shrug, bid*

C A low note: *chattering, veering, windscreen wiper dented, wing, witnessed*

D Phone home: *double-glazing, receiver, whispered*

E Signed, sealed and delivered: *trenchcoat, dog-eared, squinted, scrawl, barrel, thrusting, shoved, holdall, booty, baffled, track down*

F An unfair cop: *joyriders, serial killers, flashed, ajar, poke around, flustered, ciggies*

G Tow job: *speedchecks, taken aback, summons, crucial*

H Fitted-up wardrobe: *keep an eye on, chaps, rack his brains*

How to use the activity

Make enough copies of the eight texts, A-H, and the eight endings for the students to have one text and one ending each, with as much variety as possible in the class.

Explain the meaning of 'Urban Myths' – apocryphal stories, usually beginning: 'This happened to a friend of a friend of mine...' and told to you by acquaintances, or sometimes complete strangers, in bars.

Give each student a story and an ending. The ending should not correspond to their story! (If you prefer to play the game in small groups of eight, instead of as a whole class activity, divide the students into groups first and then give each group eight stories and endings to be shuffled and dealt out randomly.)

Students should read their story and try to write a sentence to end the story.

The object of the activity is to then find the person with the real ending to their story.

To do this, the students should walk around the class retelling their story until they meet the person who has the real ending. This person should give them the slip of paper with the ending on.

When they have found their own endings and given away their original ones, they should sit down. When everyone is sitting down, students can tell their stories to the class, comparing the endings they wrote, with the real endings.

Key: The correct endings are printed alongside the stories in the photocopiable Games material section.

Follow-up: This activity can lead into a discussion on Urban Myths – are there any such stories circulating in the students' own cultures?

9 Famous last words

Type of activity
whole class mêlée then groups of four
retelling anecdotes about famous witticisms and filling in speech bubbles

Level/Time required
intermediate/shorter than average

Games material
Introductory cartoons
Parker, Coward, Wilde, Whistler cartoons
Texts: A; B; C; D; E; F; G; H; I; J; K; L; M; N; O; P
Worksheet

Function practised
reporting what other people said

Structures
past tenses, reported speech

Lexical areas
social occasions, art, music, theatre

Problem vocabulary

Parker, Coward, Wilde, Whistler cartoons: *disaster, genius, good shot, feigning, dim-witted, impresario, blew his brains out, featuring, prodigy, engage in, would-be, insulter, foyer, rotten, customs officer, scintillating*

A: *nosey*
B: *threatened, legal action, sue*
C: *bust*
D: *son of a gun, snapped, exception*
E: *get the better of, latter, enclosing*
F: *potty*
G: *courteously*
H: *rebuked, intoxicated, sober*
I: *ill-received, stage, cabled*
J: *hostess*
K: *tone-deaf, orchestra, dominoes*
L: *would-be, pompous, scribbled*
M: *despair of, disconsolately, easel, masterpiece, perspective, alter*
N: *snapshot*
O: *afford*
P: *cabinetmaker, sketch*

How to use the activity

Make one copy of the introductory cartoons for each student. Make enough copies of the Parker, Coward, Wilde, Whistler cartoons for one half of the students to have a copy each. Make enough copies of the sixteen texts, A-P, for the students to have one text each, with as much variety as possible in the class. Make enough copies of the worksheet for one quarter of the students to have a copy each.

Begin by giving everyone a copy of the introductory cartoons and talking about them together. Find out if the students know who the people are (Sir Winston Churchill, war leader and one-liner extraordinary; George Bernard Shaw, playwright, critic, socialist; Pablo Picasso, Spanish artist, sculptor and wry wit; Groucho Marx, US comic, maker of snappy remarks) and give them a little background if they don't. If you have an overhead projector, you may prefer to copy the introductory cartoons onto an OHT for this discussion, rather than hand out copies.

Put the students into pairs and give each pair a copy of the Parker, Coward, Wilde, Whistler cartoons. Ask the students to work in pairs to match the stories with their last lines. When they have done this, give each student one of the sixteen texts, A-P. If you have fewer than sixteen students, give some students two texts. If you have more than sixteen students, some students will have the same text. Ask them to read and memorise the details of the story so that they can tell it to others.

When they are ready, ask them to get up and walk around the class telling their story to other people. You can put a time limit on this part of the activity if you like. When they have finished or the time limit is up, regroup them into fours and give each group a worksheet to fill in.

The object of the activity is to see how many exchanges they can remember and fill in.

Key: 1h, 2c, 3i, 4g, 5d, 6f, 7b, 8a, 9e. Worksheet 1 'How much are you paid?' 'Oh, I don't get paid in dollars. The lady of the house just lets me sleep with her.' 2 'Your title, *A Night in Casablanca*, is too close to our title, *Casablanca*.' 'I'll sue you for using the word "Brothers".' 3 'What do you think of the latest Victor Mature/Hedy Lamarr film?' 'You can't expect the public to get excited about a film where the leading man's bust is bigger than the leading lady's.' 4 'You old son-of-a-gun, you probably don't remember me.' 'I never forget a face but in your case I'll be glad to make an exception.' 5 'One for yourself and one for a friend – if you have one.' 'I can't make it, but can I have tickets for the second night – if there is one.' 6 'After all, they say he's potty.' 'They say he can't hear either.' 7 'I hope to photograph you again on your hundredth birthday.' 'I don't see why not. You look reasonably fit to me.' 8 'You're drunk.' 'And you, madam, are ugly. But I shall be sober tomorrow.' 9 'I will stage your play.' 'Better never than late.' 10 'Are you enjoying yourself?' 'Certainly. There is nothing else here to enjoy.' 11 'What would you like us to play next?' 'Dominoes.' 12 'Lady Blank will be at home on Tuesday between four and six o'clock.' 'Mr Bernard Shaw likewise.' 13 'It's a masterpiece.' 'No, the nose is all wrong. It throws the whole picture out of perspective.' 'Then why not alter the nose?' 'I can't find it.' 14 'I don't like modern paintings because they aren't realistic.' 'My, is she really as small as that?' 15 'Why don't you have any of your own paintings on your walls?' 'I can't afford them.' 16 'How much will it cost?' 'Nothing at all. Just sign the sketch.'

Follow-up: Ask students to imagine what would happen if Picasso met Groucho Marx or Churchill met Shaw. Who would insult the other more? Ask them to work in pairs to write an insulting dialogue.

10 Body language

Type of activity
jigsaw in four groups then groups of four
sharing information on different nationalities' gestures and completing a worksheet on body language in different countries

Level/Time required
upper intermediate/shorter than average

Games material
Texts: Introductory text; A; B; C; D
Questionnaire

Function practised
describing customs

Structures
present simple, present perfect, present continuous

Lexical areas
nationalities, gestures

Problem vocabulary

Introductory text: *light-hearted, gaffes, collide, reverse, fascinating, mingling, signals, cast, globe, rubbing shoulders, posture, gesture, body-lingo, mutually incomprehensible, unwitting, insult*

A: *cheery, thumbs up, cabbies, clonks, devastatingly, insulting, incidentally, thumb a lift, luggage trolley, on-looker, worthless rogue*

B: *give offence, assailed, tremendous, itch, tug, earlobe, insult, rotten, sponger, watch it, mate, sneaky, so-and-so, get lost, pansy, ineffably, hang around*

C: *ring-gesture, glancing, remarks, sou, enraged, obscenity, chokes, appalls, go to hell, restrained, punch, maître d', out-thrust, palms, promptly, skewers*

D: *eyelid, make a pass at, thrust, palms, gesture, descended from, smear, filth, condemned, gutter, vile, taboo, give two fingers, misinterpretation, the wonder is, functions, flattering*

How to use the activity

Copy an introductory text and a questionnaire for each student. Make enough copies of text A for one quarter of the students to have a copy each, and the same for texts B, C and D.
You might like to preface this activity with a short class discussion on body language and gestures. Demonstrate a few gestures (counting to ten, 'I don't know', 'You're crazy', etc.) and ask the students for their equivalents, if they are from a different cultural background.
Then hand out the introductory text to all students and

discuss the gestures described in it.
Divide the class into four groups, A, B, C and D. Give text A to each student in group A, text B to all those in group B, etc.
Give them time to read their text and to memorise the information it contains, while you circulate to deal with queries. Then regroup the students into fours, so that each new group contains an A, a B, a C and a D.
Ask them to share the information they have just read with the other members of the group. They should use their own words, as far as possible, without looking back at the text. If you want to make things difficult for an advanced group, tell them that no hand movements are allowed – they must explain everything in words!
The object of the activity is to collect as much information as possible in order to complete the questionnaire.
When the students have finished sharing information, give them each a copy of the questionnaire. They should complete it individually without consultation in the first instance and then, when everyone in the group has got as far as they can, they may help each other.
Students may like to see copies of all the texts at the end.

Key: 1 A 'moutza' is an insulting Greek gesture (palms up). 2 A 'Victory V' is the first two fingers held up in a V-sign (V for Victory). 3 Britain. 4 Because an outstretched thumb is insulting. 5 'Thumbs-up' in Britain means 'fine', 'OK'. 6 Go to hell. 7a Saudi Arabia. 7b South America. 8a Zero. 8b A-OK. 8c Money. 8d I'll kill you. 8e An obscenity. 9a You rotten sponger. 9b You'd better watch it. 9c You sneaky little so and so. 9d Get lost you pansy. 9e Something wonderful.

Follow-up: Write a set of guidelines for staff working at Heathrow Airport, or imagine an international misunderstanding and write the resulting dialogue.

11 Time warp

Type of activity
pairwork then groups of four
reading a text about life a hundred years ago and sharing the information

Level/Time required
upper intermediate/average

Games material
Worksheet
Texts: 50 years ago; Today; A Six in the bed; B Life was hard; C 'Children should be seen and not heard'; D Appearances

Function practised
talking about life in past times

Structures
past tenses, *would* (to express habits), *may have*

Lexical areas
work, living conditions, children's behaviour, clothes

Problem vocabulary

50 years ago: *shame, vandalism, non-existent, respected,*

issue, instil, make-believe, porridge, poultry, dull, itchy, siblings, social stigma, errands, treat, comics, three Rs, 11-plus, specifically, wireless, wring, baking

Today: differentiated, pest, menace, supplemented, well equipped, service industry, guilty, current, casual, hand-me-downs, outfit, non-issue, get away with, cheeky, misbehave, deterrent, munch, snack, take-away

A Six in the bed: crowded, a lot to do with, strict, nurseries, crêches, mill, neglecting, tragedy, communal, blunder, survive

B Life was hard: rough, survive, poultry, stagger, pail, scarcely, beloved, admired, nursing, soothe, hush, rock, dandle, distracted, conduct, guardianship, weary, sheaves, cart, line up with, gritty

C 'Children should be seen and not heard': answer back, boxed my ears, chatter, strict, behaviour, fussiness, tolerated, grace, swallowed, hasty, suet pudding and treacle, unsuitable, forbidden, slogan, dull, punishment, feature, leather, chastisement, yard, strap, strip, bruises

D Appearances: scarce, bargains, second-hand, hand-me-downs, patched, mended, swap, cropped, plait, crimped

How to use the activity

Make one copy of the worksheet for each student. Make enough copies of the text 50 years ago for half the students to have a copy each and enough copies of Today for the other half. Make enough copies of text A for one quarter of the students to have a copy each, and the same for texts B, C and D.

Ask the students for anecdotes: differences between their parents and themselves, or between themselves and younger or older brothers and sisters for example.

Then give each student the worksheet with the introductory paragraph and headings. Ask the students to talk in pairs about how they think children have changed over the last fifty years in relation to the topics on the worksheet. (This should be kept fairly brief.)

Then give one student in each pair the 50 years ago text and the other the Today text. Ask them to match the headings on the worksheet with the paragraphs in their text. When they have finished, ask them to share their information with their partner.

Then ask the pairs to join up together into groups of four. Give each student in the group a different text (A, B, C or D) describing children's life a hundred years ago. Ask them to complete part two of the worksheet, first choosing the headings that apply to their text and then making brief notes under each heading, on the back of their worksheet. When they have done this, get them to tell the others in the group about their life.

The object of the activity is to imagine they are a child of a century ago and to tell the others about their life.

Key: 50 years ago – clothes f, games d, money g, transport h, home a, holidays b, discipline c, bedtime k, food e, music j, school i; Today – clothes h, games i, money c, transport b, home d, holidays g, discipline j, bedtime a, food k, music e, school f

Follow-up: Write a letter from a child fifty years ago to a child now.

12 Curious customs

Type of activity
whole class mêlée
finding out about traditional customs and filling in a calendar

Level/Time required
upper intermediate/average

Games material
Texts: A New Year's Day; B Shrove Tuesday; C Kissing Friday; D April Fool's Day; E May Day; F Halloween; G Mischief Night; H New Year's Eve
Worksheet

Function practised
describing habits and customs

Structures
present simple

Lexical areas
customs and rituals

Problem vocabulary

A New Year's Day: rise, make the round, mincepies, fool

B Shrove Tuesday: festival, pancake, fair, cane, skipping, blocked, lengths, clothesline, abreast

C Kissing Friday: mixed class, embarrassment, lad, proved, encountered, expostulate, turmoil

D April Fool's Day: joyous, hoax, pigeon, come in for their share, fooling, needlework, taken in, exempt, glueing, stuck, yell, eggshell, sense of humour, fright

E May Day: maidens, rise, dawn, dew, ensure, complexion, pimples, freckles, customary, rite, thereafter, maypole, garlands, stool, lace curtain

F Halloween: tub, basin, floated, stab, hook, nail, cored, supernatural influences, peel, initial, represents, stands for, vigorously, row, part

G Mischief Night: mischief, hooliganism, lawlessness, permissible, assaulted, bogus, hoisted, daubed, coated, treacle, tripped over, unscrewed, tapped, drainpipes, stuffed, set alight, wet through, ashes, loop, door knobs, tugging

H New Year's Eve: ashes, afresh, assist, wealth, health, household, first-footer, welcomed, hospitality, threshold, ensure, well-being, spirit, siren, sprig, evergreen, toast (drink)

How to use the activity

Make enough copies of text A for one eighth of the students to have a copy each, and the same for texts B – H.
Make enough copies of the worksheet for a quarter of the class.
Begin by asking students about customs and rituals on special days in their countries. (This is a good activity to do either on a day when it is one of their own festivals, or on a British festival, or as part of a British Life and Institutions course.)
Divide the class into eight groups, A, B, C, D, E, F, G and H. Give text A to each student in group A, text B to those in group B, etc.

Tell them they are going to read abut customs that take place on certain festival days in Britain. Give the groups time to read their text and discuss it. Go round and help as necessary.

When they have finished, ask them all to stand up.

The object of the activity is to find out as much as possible about customs that take place on other festival days.

To do this they will have to move around the class telling each other about their day and the rituals that happen on it. When they have finished or the time limit (10–15 minutes) is up, put them in groups of four and give each group a worksheet. They should work together to complete the worksheet, filling in the calendar with the names of the days and the activities and customs that happen on those days. Round off the activity by going through the calendar and asking what happens on each day.

Key: January – New Year's Day, children ask for gifts; February – Shrove Tuesday, people make and throw pancakes, everyone goes skipping, a bell is rung; February – Kissing Friday, boys can kiss any girl they like; April – April Fool's Day, children tell people things that aren't true, children play tricks on grown-ups; May – May Day, girls wash their faces in the dew, children visit houses with garlands of flowers; October – Halloween, girls put nuts in the fire, girls brush their hair in front of the mirror, children play duck apple, girls throw apple peel over their shoulder; November – Mischief Night, children play tricks on grown-ups; December – New Year's Eve, people place money and bread outside the door, householders welcome a tall dark man with wood, coal and silver coins.

Follow up: Ask students to write a description of a festival day and its customs from their own country.

13 Village gossip

Type of activity
whole class mêlée (minimum of 8) then pairwork retelling information from a document about village history and filling in a questionnaire

Level/Time required
upper intermediate/longer than average

Games material
Village map
Texts: A Grey House; B Rose Cottage; C Hazel Cottage; D Manor Farm; E Willow Cottage; F Honeysuckle Cottage; G Annie's Cottage; H Swallow Cottage
Questionnaire

Function practised
narrating past events

Structures
past tenses

Lexical areas
village life: love, crime, school, church, quarrels, ghosts, weddings

Problem vocabulary

A Grey House: *misdoings, involve, prominent, linked, bring charges, break-in, culminated, kidnapped, ransom, unavailable for comment, coma, consciousness*

B Rose Cottage: *grace, melt, grateful, volunteered, charabanc, smocking, outing, Reverend, eloquent, combination, spiritual wholesomeness, masculinity, fluttering, refrained, parish, blush, enhanced, choir practice*

C Hazel Cottage: *benefit, explorations, forte, timekeeping, common factor, breadth, precocious, verbal dexterity, inestimable, rarity, instinctive, skill, unequalled, forays, brace, harvest, necessitates, prolonged*

D Manor Farm: *heartfelt, token, benighted, ablaze, chapel, peal, echo, oak, pews, flock, blessed, ailments, weaving, exquisite, hassocks, fellowship*

E Willow Cottage: *insurrection, rebellion, sedition, parishioners, combat, slain, pistol, pierced, wounded, duelling, outlawed, settle, disputes, baptized, font, upstanding, length and breadth, upbringing, naught, fled, distress, betwixt, ghosts, haunted, revelation, presence, glimpsed, apparition, pistol, vanishing, duel*

F Honeysuckle Cottage: *decade*

G Annie's Cottage: *fitfully, treat, cruel, hard-hearted, means, disposal, witness, deceived, depth, suffer, dragged through the mire, scandal, gossip, unworthy*

H Home Farm: *out of sorts, wedding breakfast, gallon, undercoat, gloss*

How to use the activity

Make one copy of the village map for each student. Make enough copies of the eight texts, A-H, for the students to have one text each. Play this game with at least eight students, so that you can ensure that someone in the class has information about a character/home. (If you have more than eight students, some texts will be duplicated – this doesn't matter, two or more people can live in the same house. You can group people living at the same address together if you like.) Make enough copies of the questionnaire to give one to each pair for the pairwork. You might like to begin with a discussion about neighbours and community life. How well do students know their neighbours? Were people friendlier in the past? Give everyone a map of the village and explain that they all live in this village. Then give out one text to each student. Explain that they found this document in the attic of the house where they live and that it gives some information about the previous occupants of the house.

Give them some time to read and absorb the information and go round and help as necessary. Then ask them to stand up and move around the class, telling the other members of the village about the juicy details they have discovered.

The object of the activity is to build up a picture of who lived where in the 1920s and to fill in their maps with names and descriptions of who lived and what happened in each house.

When the students have finished listening to each others' stories, put them in pairs and give each pair a questionnaire to fill in.

Key: a Grey House; b Rose Cottage; c Swallow Cottage, Annie's Cottage; d Hazel Cottage; e The Old Rectory; f Manor Farm; g Home Farm; h Willow Cottage; i Church Cottage; j Honeysuckle Cottage; k Willow Cottage

Follow up: Ask students to imagine who lived in Manor Farm, the Old Barn and Church Cottage and to write documents containing scandal or gossip about their inhabitants.

14 A life in the day

Type of activity
whole class mêlée then pair work
retelling a description of a half day's work to find the person with the other half

Level/Time required
upper intermediate/average

Games material
Texts: A; B; C; D; E; F
Information sheet
Photos

Function practised
describing daily routines

Structures
present simple, passive

Lexical areas
work, leisure, hobbies

Problem vocabulary

A: *fiendish attachment, aromatic, vignettes, nonsense, well brought-up, disarray, efficiency, grace, vying, dominance, deny, unsolicited, fabulous, zucchini*

B: *issue, chit-chat, minimalised, sensual gratification, longhand, disbelief, suspended, indulgence*

C: *bull, take advantage, flatter, contours, macho, responsibility, glory, stress, foolish, shocked, tossed, ribs, react*

D: *superstitious, touch-up, dangling, criticism, failure, risk, administration, logistics, calamities, recurring nightmares*

E: *exhausted, muck out, cereal, incentive, irritating, treatment, tack*

F: *invoices, debts, chap, tougher, effective, legal action, mucking out, cosmetics, shattered*

How to use the activity

Make enough copies of the six texts, A-F, for the students to have one text each, with as much variety as possible in the class. Copy one information sheet for each student. Make enough copies of the sets of photos for half the class to have one each, or alternatively one set to display on the wall.
Each of the texts, A-F, represents half a day (either up to or after lunchtime) in the life of one of the three characters in the photos.
Begin with a short discussion on what time of day the students like best and why.

Give each student one text, ensuring that as far as possible students get different texts. Try to ensure too, that each student has a partner somewhere in the class, with the other half of the day. If you have an odd number of students, there will be one group of three rather than a pair.
Give each student an information sheet and ask them to read their text and fill in the information sheet as far as possible, although there will be some questions that they cannot answer at this stage. While they are doing this, circulate and deal with any problems and queries.
When they have finished, ask them to stand up and walk around the class, telling other people about their lifestyle, hobbies and habits.
The object of the activity is to find someone who they think is their 'other half'.
When they find this person, they should check with you and then, if they are correct, they should go and sit together and find out in detail how the missing half of the day is spent, completing their information sheets.
Finally, give each pair a set of photos and ask them to identify which character is theirs. Alternatively you could display one set of photos for all the students to look at.

Key: A and B, C and D, E and F.

Follow-up: Get students to write a letter or a diary entry from the character, or imagine a dialogue between two of the characters.

15 Guilty secrets

Type of activity
jigsaw in five groups then groups of five
retelling an anecdote and discussing reactions to it

Level/Time required
upper intermediate/average

Games material
Texts: A Headmaster; B Novelist; C Writer; D Journalist; E Cartoonist
Worksheet

Function practised
narrating past experiences

Structures
past tenses

Lexical areas
daily life: love, marriage, school, babycare, feelings, emotions

Problem vocabulary

A Headmaster: *headmaster, sin, essay, biography, moral, heading, resist, cheat, guilty, error, arch rival, unbearable, anthology*

B Novelist: *astonishing, ravaged, nap, snack, extract, gush, compound, dilemma, cot, desperate, howling, choked, glance, staggered, circumstances, dreadlocks, hesitation, palms, dabble, gratitude, lick*

C Writer: *series, receptive, sheer, tenacity, persistent, yell, inevitable, giggled, automatically, Pavlovian, insistent*

D Journalist: *swaggering, the coast was clear, grandly, sinking heart, abuse, electoral register, painstakingly, desperate, personnel manager, deputy, documents, dial, assignment*

E Cartoonist: *shin, characteristics, kick, crumpled, self-pity, ruin, threw up, reaction, hop, stool, consume, top up with, peer, letter flap, agony, casualty, grave, shamefacedly, limp, in plaster, haste, rival, trip*

How to use the activity

Make enough copies of the five texts, A-E, for the students to have one text each, with as much variety as possible in the class. Copy one worksheet for each student.

You might like to begin by telling the class a short anecdote about something embarrassing that happened to you. Unless your class know each other very well/are pretty uninhibited, it is probably better not to ask for personal revelations from them at this point!

Divide the class into five groups, A, B, C, D and E. Give text A to each student in group A, text B to all those in group B, etc. Give each student a worksheet.

Ask the students to read their text and complete section A of their worksheet, while you circulate and deal with any problems and queries. When they have finished, ask the students in each group to talk about their reactions to the incident: to discuss what the character involved felt at the time and how he/she feels about the incident now, comparing their answers on the worksheet. Then regroup the students into fives, so that each new group contains an A, a B, a C, a D and an E.

The object of the activity is for the students to tell their stories to each other as if the experience had happened to them, and to fill in section B of their worksheet as they are listening to the others.

After each anecdote the students should compare reactions.

Key: Answers will vary.

Follow-up: Students could write about a similar personal experience, or if they don't feel like doing this, write a diary entry for one of the characters for the day the incident occurred.

16 Loose morals

Type of activity
whole class mêlée then pairs
retelling a fable and finding the appropriate moral

Level/Time required
upper intermediate/average

Games material
Texts: A The crow; B The mice; C The ass (1); D The ass (2); E The dove; F The bear; G The tortoise; H The maid; I The miser; J The lion

Function practised
narrating a story

Structures
past tenses

Lexical areas
animals

Problem vocabulary

A The crow: *crow, pitcher, relieved, swiftly, stooped, strained, thereupon, overturn, alas, pebbles, creep, brim, quench, carry out*

B The mice: *ridding, rejected, tyrant, necessity, invention*

C The ass (1): *ass, humble, track, rounding a bend, bog, stumbling, clumsily, frantic, struggling, sink, mud, amidst, horde, leaping, woe, groaned, bray, piteously, sigh, splashed, mire, fuss, confidence, disaster*

D The ass (2): *ass, fruitless, hunting, padded, plump, foolishly, munching ,crunching, briar, perched, stile, rangy, cock, crowing, offended, bounded, haste, idly, plucked, galloped, mere, jungle, error, custom, familiar*

E The dove: *dove, ant, bubbling, blade, slipped, current, snatched, struggling, pity, distress, branch, delay, clambered, nimbly, stroll, trap, net, heel, take fright, misfortune, sincerity*

F The bear: *face to face with, fear, single-handed, match for, sniffing, courage, held his breath, perch, wisely, leave in the lurch, good turn*

G The tortoise: *tortoise, eagle, dusty, wheeling, circling, dissatisfied, long to, freedom, soar, swoop, ponder, discontented, enviously, seizing, favourable, opportunity, treasures, monarch, declined, task, absurd, pressed by, entreaties, height, loose, hold, bidding, misguided, dashed to pieces, hatched*

H The maid: *milkmaid, balancing, prospects, a tidy price, stock, spoil, gown, grand, seek out, shrug, toss, toppled, smashed, spilt, trickled, dust, overambitious, destroy*

I The miser: *miser, mean, goods, property, melted, solid, mass, buried, hoard, gloat, spy on, villain, went out of his mind, loss, crowd*

J The lion: *weakness, prey, den, condition, concern, beasts, pay respects, wily, lair, renowned, cunning, consolation, bless you, uneasy, footsteps, emerging, riches*

How to use the activity

Make enough copies of the ten texts, A-J, for the students to have one different text each. If you have more than ten students, play the game in two or more groups. If you have fewer than ten students in the class or group, leave out one or more of the pairs of texts (A/B, C/D, E/F, G/H, I/J). (If you have an odd number of students a loose moral will be unavoidable! You will end up with one group of three instead of a pair.)

Tell the students they are going to read fables or moral tales, mostly about animals. Ask them if they can think of proverbs or sayings from their cultures which involve animals, e.g. the early bird catches the worm.

Give each student a text and ask them to read the story and memorise the details for retelling, while you circulate and help with problems or difficulties.

When they have finished, tell them that the moral at the bottom of the story is not the right moral for that story. They should walk around the class, telling their fable to other students.

The object of the activity is to find another student who has a story which fits their moral.

The students should not tell anyone their morals until they have found the right story.

Key: The 'moral exchange' is reciprocal – i.e. if a student's moral fits another student's story, their moral will fit the original story. The pairs of stories are A and B, C and D, E and F, G and H, I and J.

Follow-up: Students write a fable to illustrate the moral they originally had.

17 Roots

Type of activity
jigsaw in three groups then groups of three
reading and retelling old family letters and completing a family tree

Level/Time required
Texts A and B:upper intermediate; Text C is easier/ longer than average

Games material
Family tree
Role cards: Karen, Gary, Lucy, Alex, Tracey, Jason
Texts: A Lily's will/Accompanying letter; B Cutting from the Pennine Bugle/Letter; C Letter

Function practised
talking about past events

Structures
past tenses

Lexical areas
family history, character, emotions

Problem vocabulary

A Lily's will: *will, estate, arable, grazing, in my name, funeral expenses, death duties, exception, expression, carbolic soap, foul, cookpot, bethink, kettle, investments, in trust, capital*

Accompanying letter: *I am not long for this world, in my bones, set the record straight, up to you, squabbling, bickering, the hereafter, set eyes on, treat, pack, heartache, inherit, fellsides, strength of character, property, memorial, rejected, pettiness, meanness, soured, raise a family, foolish, pride, humility, virtuous, respect, shed tears*

B Cutting from the Pennine Bugle: *scandal, detained, undercover regiment, den of corruption, sheeprustling network, issue, statement, charges, persistence, decade, unprecedented, investigations, stockbreeders, traders, acre, currently, alleged, rationing, widespread, black market, slaughter houses, accomplice, revolving round, barracks, magistrate's court*

Letter: *operation, teething, worn out, clearing up, lining, capable of, fishy, blossom, folk, torture, bear to, set eyes on, owes*

C Letter: *fells, a wink of sleep, overdue, another living soul, pregnant, on account of, in the family way, bore a child, out of wedlock, jealousy, barren, stroke, quarrelsome*

How to use the activity
Make enough copies of the family tree for the students to have one each. Make enough copies of each of the six role cards for one sixth of the students to have a copy each.

Make enough copies of text A for one third of the students to have a copy each, and the same for texts B and C.
Ask students how far back they can name people from their family. How much do they know about their ancestors?
Divide the class into three groups, A, B, and C. Within each group divide the students into pairs so that as far as possible everyone is working with a partner.
Tell the students that they all come from a large family, and the three groups they are in represent three different branches of the family. Unfortunately, because of some old family feuds, the three branches do not know each other. Their task is to find out as much as possible about their ancestors and discover what happened in the past.
Give each student a copy of the family tree and a role card as follows:
Group A pairs: Karen, Gary
Group B pairs: Lucy, Alex
Group C pairs: Tracey, Jason
Give them some time to read their card and to fill in their family tree with as much information as possible. They can discuss and compare notes in their pairs.
Then tell them that some documents about their family have recently come to light: group A have found an old will and letter (text A), group B have found a newspaper cutting with note attached (text B), and group C have an old unposted letter (text C). Give each group copies of the relevant text. Allow them time to read and discuss the texts and to complete the family tree as far as possible. Go round and give help as required.
When they have finished, regroup the students into threes, so that each new group contains an A, a B, and a C.
The object of the activity is to tell each other what family scandals they have unearthed, and to finish completing their family trees.

Key:

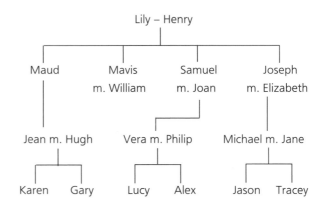

Follow-up: Write letters to other members of their family saying what they have found out, and offering to forget the past.

18 Ghost stories

Type of activity
two groups then pairwork
retelling a ghost story and finding the ending

Level/Time required
upper intermediate/longer than average

Games material
Texts: On the Brighton road; The clock
Endings: A, B

Function practised
narrating a story

Structures
past tenses

Lexical areas
house, landscape

Problem vocabulary

On the Brighton road: *downs, sparkling, blended, keenness, alternation, vacant, limbs, grimly, loitered, stooping, huskily, lonesome, limping, casually, dog-tired, knocking about, hay, smack in your face, lurched, doubtfully, strained, pneumonia, workhouse, winked, vanished*

The clock: *waylaid, bounded, flagged, conveys, quilts, vibration, mechanism, motion, indentation, reluctantly, capacious, pull myself together, winding-screw, running down, fumble, hopping, scratching*

A: *splashed, thawing, begged, crept, trudging, slushy, fragile, aghast*

B: *grip, negotiated, sash-window, fainting fit*

How to use the activity

Make enough copies of the text 'On the Brighton road' and ending B for half the students in your class and enough copies of the text 'The clock' and ending A for the other half. Begin by asking the students if they believe in ghosts. Do they know any ghost stories?

Divide the class into two groups, A and B. Give each student in group A a copy of the text 'On the Brighton road' and give each student in group B 'The clock'. If you have a large class, subdivide the two large groups into smaller groups to read and discuss the story. Tell them their stories are incomplete and ask them to think up a suitably chilling ending to the story.

When they have discussed this, give each student in group A a copy of the ending to the other group's story (ending B) and each student in group B a copy of ending A. Ask them to discuss what they think came before it.

Then regroup the students in pairs, so that each pair contains an A and a B, and ask them to retell their stories. **The object of the activity is for each to contribute the ending to the other's story.**

Which were better, the real endings or their imagined ones?

Key: On the Brighton road – A; The Clock – B

Follow-up: Students could write their own ghost stories. It might help to stimulate their imagination if you give them a list of elements to include, e.g. an old house, a portrait of an old gentleman, a bell, a creaking floorboard, a locked room. Alternatively, you could bring in a set of 'props': an old photo, a train ticket, a lace handkerchief, a pipe, etc.

19 Murder in the library

Type of activity
jigsaw in three groups then groups of three
retelling a story and solving a murder mystery

Level/Time required
upper intermediate/longer than average

Games material
Texts: A What the butler saw; B What the maid heard;
C What the vicar felt
Worksheet

Functions practised
narration, hypothesis

Structures
past tenses, conditionals, *could have, might have, may have, can't have*

Lexical areas
character, emotions

Problem vocabulary

A What the butler saw: *parlour, furious, flirting, intimate, port, appealingly, surreptitiously, billiard room, ballroom, glimpse, urgent, piercing, gasped, fainted, decanter, smashed, stubs, candlestick, conservatory, unconscious, rushing*

B What the maid heard: *formal, row, cast off, sobbing, rushed, slammed, overhearing, mean, gambling, short of money, peeped, dashing, velvet, look like thunder, passionately, intimate, broke up, retired, embarrassed, muttered, murder, footsteps, piercing, gasped, fainted*

C What the vicar felt: *confide in, express, congratulate, affect, will, in favour of, conscious, strained, atmosphere, tiff, thundercloud, broach the subject, endeavoured, anecdote, retire, snooker, urgent, port, parlour, distasteful, stroll, composing, slamming, grunted, strode, shrubbery, chime, terrace, aware, flash, strike*

How to use the activity

Make enough copies of text A for one third of the students to have a copy each, and the same for texts B and C. Make one copy of the worksheet for each student.

Give the class a little background to the story: a murder happened in a country house last night. They are going to read an account of what happened from the point of view of someone who was there at the time: the butler, the maid or the vicar.

Divide the class into three groups, A, B and C. Give text A to each student in group A, text B to all those in group B and text C to all those in group C. Give out the same worksheet to all the students, but tell them that they will not be able to complete all the questions on the worksheet, so not to worry if they find something they can't answer.

Give them some time to work on the text together in their groups, while you go round explaining vocabulary, dealing with queries, etc. Then regroup the students into threes, so that each new group contains an A, a B and a C.

Ask them to tell their stories to each other as if they were the butler, the maid and the vicar, and to help each other to complete the worksheet.

The object of the activity is to then find out who the murderer was.

Note: This activity will probably take the whole lesson. If the students haven't found the right solution by the end of the lesson, you might like to offer a small prize for the first correct solution by the next class and let them go on puzzling at home.

Key: 1 kitchen – Velvet, dining room, parlour – old Archibald, Myrtle Berry and Dame Christie, staircase, hall – Charlotte, terrace – Jeffery (garden) and Reverend Truelove, conservatory – Daphne and young Archibald, library – Miss Topless?, Mrs Horsehair (the body), billard room – Mr Oscarsson and Miss Topless?, ballroom – Miss Topless?. 2 Charlotte – the maid, Velvet – the butler, Reverend Truelove – the local vicar, Mildred Horsehair – a rich widow in her 40s (the owner of the house), Daphne – the niece, Jeffery – the son, Oscar Oscarsson – an influential but impoverished film director, young Archibald – a dashing but penniless young man, old Archibald – a neighbour, Myrtle Berry – an American lady, Agatha Christie – a lady novelist, Alice B. Topless – an actress. 3 Daphne and young Archibald might murder Mrs Horsehair because Daphne would lose her inheritance if she married young Archibald; Jeffery because he would lose his inheritance if his mother married Oscarsson; Miss Topless because she was jealous of Mrs Horsehair's relationship with Oscarsson. Solution – The murderer was Alice B. Topless. She was the only one wearing blue who was alone and unobserved at 10.00 p.m. (Daphne was with Archibald in the conservatory and Jeffery left the house by the front door a minute or so before the murder.) Mrs Horsehair left the ballroom after a row with Oscarsson and Topless and went to the library, where she had another row with Jeffery, who left the house by the front door. Miss Topless came in by the billard room door, hit Mrs Horsehair on the head with a candlestick and left, with the murder weapon, by the window. In the grounds she found the vicar and hit him over the head too with the candlestick. She then went back into the house by the front door. Her motive was jealousy of Oscarsson's relationship with Mrs Horsehair.

Follow-up: Students could write a police report giving the reasoning behind the arrest of Miss Topless, a police interview with Miss Topless, a newspaper interview with one of the characters or a newspaper report on the murder.

20 Believe it or not

Type of activity
whole class mêlée then pairs or groups
retelling information about the paranormal and completing a worksheet

Level/Time required
upper intermediate/longer than average

Games material
Texts: Introductory text; A Bermuda triangle; B Corn circles; C Cryptozoology; D UFOs; E Cold reading; F Psychic detectives; G Telepathy; H Biorhythms
Worksheet

Function practised
defining and explaining, justifying, giving reasons

Structures
various past and present tenses, *would*

Lexical areas
the supernatural

Problem vocabulary

Introductory text: *fiver, adept, sleight of hand, hoaxers, sceptic, tambourine, tabloid, peddling, gullible*

A Bermuda triangle: *kicking round, allegedly, mysteriously, without trace, flying saucers, crews, astral, embellished, inaccurate, explicable, all-time favourite, manned, peril, compass, malfunctioned, guidance, promulgators*

B Corn circles: *corn circles, visible, hoaxers, battier, fake, outer space, fairyland, self-confessed, by the same token, elves, Santa, anguishing, psychic, aliens*

C Cryptozoology: *non-existent, mysterious, scintilla, untraceable, suspiciously, duplicate, hoaxes, otters, serpent, deer, refraction, atmospheric, flipper, monster, prehistoric, extrapolated, retouched, computer-enhanced, vastness, incapable, shambling, orang-utan*

D UFOs: *littering, alien, refracted, haze, regrettably, civilian, spot (= see), skipped, experimental psychologist, civilisations, galaxy, infrequent, conquer, investigating, claimed, subsequent, invisible, entities*

E Cold reading: *technique, innumerable, charlatans, palmists, fortune tellers, spiritualists, astrologers, cunning, acute observation, suspension, scepticism, fraud, parlayed, medium, session, mass gathering, inevitably, turned to her advantage, rotten, fake, cosy, distressed, miraculous, mightily, blamed, lines crossed, goodwill, scorned, spectacularly, powerful, occasion*

F Psychic detectives: *forensic, high-profile, bogged down, medium, credits herself, pursuit, arrested, killer, bore no resemblance to, wrought iron, victim, mercifully, validated, endorse, evidence*

G Telepathy: *limited, knowledge, educated guess, smugly, wonder, consistency, amateurs, mindreaders, initially, conditions, invariably, stringent, mentalist, odd (number), digit, survey*

H Biorhythms: *dominated, cycle, calculator, alleged, the reverse, common factor, peak, researchers, survives, quoted, proponents, cash in on, subject to, jet lag, menstrual cycle, phenomena, advocates, citing, specific, tournaments, evidence*

How to use the activity

Make enough copies of the introductory text and worksheet for each student. Make enough copies of the eight texts, A-H, for the students to have one text each, with as much variety as possible in the class.

Give everyone in the class a copy of the introductory text. Ask them as quickly as possible to list:

1. The examples given of paranormal wonders
2. The examples given of rational scientific wonders
3. Reasons for not accepting paranormal phenomena

Collect suggestions and draw up three lists on the board. You may like to have a short introductory discussion based on the class list of paranormal wonders: what do they feel are possible rational explanations for these phenomena? Keep the discussion brief at this stage.

Give out one text to each student, ensuring that as many different texts as possible are used. Give everyone a copy of the worksheet and ask them to read their text and complete the worksheet for their text. While they are reading, move around the class dealing with problems as they arise.

When everyone seems to have finished, ask them all to get up and move around the class asking for information about paranormal phenomena.

The object of the activity is to get enough information to complete their worksheets.

When they have completed their worksheet they should sit down and compare their results with the person sitting next to them. When most people have finished, put them into groups of three or four and ask them to discuss the various phenomena listed on the worksheet: who believes in what? Do they accept the paranormal explanation or the scientific one?

Key: A i) An area of sea where planes and ships disappear; ii) many disasters documented, e.g. flight 19 – 5 planes vanished for no reason; iii) lieutenant unfamiliar with area, two compasses malfunctioned, lost with too little fuel. B i) Circles appearing in crop fields; ii) many appear in fields; iii) twelve teams created circles at night proving they could be done by hoaxers. C i) Study of mysterious creatures e.g. Loch Ness monster, yeti; ii) photos and sightings of 'Nessie'; iii) photos could be duplicated with models or computer enhanced negatives, yeti could be a bear. D i) Unidentified flying objects; ii) many accounts, e.g. Arnold (47) saw a moving object, Adamski met a Venusian; iii) most solar systems are 200 light years away, this would make visits very infrequent. E i) Dead people speaking through a medium; ii) listeners are impressed, messages seem to be for them; iii) general statements are made which could apply to anyone, some guesses are inevitably correct, Mrs Stokes' husband relayed information to her, customer has paid money and is anxious to succeed. F i) Psychics assist with police enquiries; ii) mediums do seem to strike lucky, e.g. Nella Jones drew a killer's face and described where he worked and lived and predicted two more murders; iii) her drawing bore no resemblance and she was wrong about the address and the murders. G i) Communication between two people without using the five senses; ii) 25% of Americans claim to have a telepathic experience, e.g. knowing who is on the phone; iii) it is not surprising we can occasionally guess who is calling, we tend to forget wrong guesses, not a single repeatable controlled experiment has been performed. H i) Our lives are dominated by three fixed cycles which begin on our birthday; ii) allegedly tested by three researchers; iii) all evidence stolen, a 1979 study found no evidence.

Follow-up: Students could write a summary of all the information they have collected, based on the notes on their worksheet.

21 Trouble with men, frogs, shoes and sisters

Type of activity
whole class mêlée then four small groups then pairwork retelling part of a story and finding the other sections

Level/Time required
upper intermediate/longer than average

Games material
Texts: A The frog prince; B The frog maiden; C Cinderella; D Beauty and Pock Face

Function practised
narrating a fairystory

Structures
various past tenses

Lexical areas
magic, home life

Problem vocabulary

A The frog prince: *gloomy, midst, foliage, fountain, wearisome, weep, melt, stretching, paddler, pearls, playfellow, chattering, croaking, dipped, seizing, hastily, giant, hopped, obliged, relish, despised, passion, consent, condemned, woe, sorrow, bound, restored*

B The frog maiden: *ill-treating, ceremony, raiment, mockingly, adamant, posy, jasmine, expectantly, hermit, deer, task, rubbed, pleaded, heir, powdering, chamber, maiden, successor, accede to*

C Cinderella: *guardian angel, maiden, dazzling, drapery, evil-minded, malicious, envious, obliged, scorn, ashes, smutty, cinders, fair, twig, tears, weep, perch, ball, trim, begged, shovelful, seeds, doves, twittering, swarm, fret, disgrace, glittering, bound, dingy, gilded, stratagem, strewed, pitch, proclamation, rage, disregarded, contrived*

D Beauty and Pock Face: *pock marks, spoilt, hemp, stack, mass, seeds, flesh, smashed, crack, slipped off, ditch, dismount, quandary, stink, scholar, merchant, pay respects to, attentive, well, shove, lost consciousness, suffering, smallpox, delicacies, deception, monster, disown, tender, console, weeping, sparrow, mystified, shoots, bamboo, ulcer, pricked, clasped, dispersed, soul, entrails, embroidered, maddened, grumble, spirit, scratch, cauldron*

How to use the activity

Make one copy of each of the four fairytales, A-D, and cut them up into as many sections as there are students in your class, trying to ensure a roughly equal number of sections per story. For example, if you have twenty students, cut each story into five approximately equal sections, if you have twelve students, cut each story into three and so on. The numbers in brackets at the end of sections of the texts (3, 4 or 5) indicate where to cut them for different numbers of students.

Begin by asking the students *What is a fairytale?* What are the main elements of a fairytale.

Give out the story sections at random so that students have one section each and give them time to read their section and ask you any questions if necessary.

The object of the first activity is to try to get into four groups corresponding to the four stories.

Tell the students that they have sections from four different stories. Do not give them the titles of the stories at this stage, but tell them that one student in each group will know the title of the story. They will have to move around the room telling other students about the characters in their story and maybe the gist of what is in their section.

Emphasise that they should do this as briefly as possible, only giving the barest essential information to enable them to decide which story they belong to.

When they have got into four groups, you can ask each group to tell the others the title of their story. Some students may want to change groups at this stage.

Then ask them to retell their section of the story to the others in the group. They should not read it out but retell the events in their own words. (Some students may decide they should be in a different story at this point too!)

The object of the activity is to place themselves in an order corresponding to the order of the sections in the story, and then retell the whole story from the beginning to check.

When they have arrived at what they think is the correct order they may like to place their slips of paper on the ground and read the story through to check.

Finally, merge the four groups into two, putting groups A and B (The frog prince and The frog maiden) together and groups C and D (Cinderella and Beauty and Pock Face) together. Ask the students to get into pairs with someone with a different story and tell each other their story.

Key: The sections of the stories go together as on the original Games material pages.

Follow-up: Give the students elements of a fairytale (e.g. a snake, egg, magic key, forest, prince, castle, etc.) and ask them to make up their own. Alternatively, ask them to choose one of the four fairytales and to 'modernise' it: how could it be updated?

22 Horoscope exchange

Type of activity
whole class mêlée
retelling a horoscope, and looking for someone who can tell you your own

Level/Time required
advanced/average

Games material
Texts: Western horoscopes – Aries, Taurus, Gemini, Cancer, Leo, Virgo, Libra, Scorpio, Sagittarius, Capricorn, Aquarius, Pisces; Chinese horoscopes – Rat, Ox, Tiger, Hare, Dragon, Snake, Horse, Sheep, Monkey, Rooster, Dog, Pig
Worksheet

Function practised
talking about character and emotions

Structures
present simple, *may, will,* imperative

Lexical areas
character, emotions

Problem vocabulary

Aries: *paradox, rash, conventional, idealistic, hard-headed, abrupt, arrogant, frank, charge, trample, daisy, self-doubt, conflict, halting, passion, expertise, plodding, statistics, uncommunicative, layabouts*

Taurus: *sensualists, domain, coerce, cross someone, earthquake, stubborn, ponderous, persistent, conduct, capacity, rage, demolition, tenacity, hustle, fair-weather friends, pushy*

Gemini: *different as chalk and cheese, duality, two-faced, wits, affable, gregarious, chilly, disgruntled, profile, insatiable, urge, restless, skim, glibly, gaily, versatility, hung-up, illogical*

Cancer: *swirling, ebbing and flowing, calculate the odds, gruff, judicious, caution, stops them in their tracks, perspicacity, exceptional, immerse, unwavering, tenacity, inquisitive, capricious, untrustworthy, rebuff*

Leo: *benevolent, despot, lordly, conduct, patronizing, superiority, flattery, pompously, snobbishly, posturing, mean-spirited, petty, lunatic, extravagance, inhibited, being dictated to, outdo*

Virgo: *purists, loners, impeccable, judgement, reserved, down-to-earth, industry (= hard work), keen intellect, dedication, trim, immaculate, diligent, methodically, objectives, dedication, pretentious, pomposity*

Libra: *predictability, unsophisticated, device, tactful, conduct, defect, superficiality, inharmonious, pride, passion, elegant, perfectly tuned, harmony, discourteous, freakish, inconsistent, unjust*

Scorpio: *misunderstood, ruthless, intensity, count the cost, mysterious, hunches, intuition, compelling, revenge, loyal, thrive, victory, motivating, stuffy, insincerity, deliberately*

Sagittarius: *crude, unbridled, tact, delicacy, superficial, touchy, jovial, breezy, exuberance, frosty, undemocratic, gloomy*

Capricorn: *one-track mind, prestige, financial recognition, materialistic, illustrate, trim, wiry, endurance, survival, agility, persevering, motivating, tradition, talk down to, irresponsible, frivolous, nag*

Aquarius: *idealist, melt, shocked, cheerily, hard facts, altruistic, spontaneous, utopian, eccentrically, individualistic, inventiveness, motivating, spirit, orthodoxy, conventional standards*

Pisces: *conflicting forces, spiritual, idealism, tentative, hesitant, conduct, vague, defect, worldliness, intensity, misplaced, motivating, intolerance*

Rat: *adaptable, creative, flair, inventiveness, quick-witted, sociable, ostentatiousness, appealing, crafty, opportunist, erratic, budgeting, scarce, lavishly*

Ox: *steadfast, methodical, suspicious, untried, unproven, reliable, take the initiative, dependable, authority, administrative, flair, unromatic, select (adj), acquaintances, loyal, possessive, prosperity, risk, logical, resolute, practicality, endurance, routine, patience*

Tiger: *competitive, easily influenced, authority, disputed, stimulant, novel (= new), paraded, bravery, rashness, impetuosity, hall-marks, ardent, restrained, convention, streak, personnel, manner*

Hare: *established, reserved, withdrawn, submissive, humble, confrontations, benevolent, clear-sightedness, judge, instinct, sincerity, sensing, falsehood, healers*

Dragon: *exotic, flamboyantly, extrovert, elegant, forefront, fertile, dream up, schemes, practical, despair, chaos, fragments, abandoned, decisive, spectacular gains, offset, adulation, the bright lights, seek out, sphere (= area)*

Snake: *by no means, pushy, adept, averse to, double-dealing, scandal, to be above something, aptitude, research, detection, academia, analytical*

Horse: *overawed, worship, disdain, relate to, team effort, gang, force, liaison*

Sheep: *affection, trust, caring, selflessness, craftsmanship, originality, complacent, confrontation, diplomatic, aggression, operates, crisis, guidance, voluntarily*

Monkey: *inventive, agile, insatiable curiosity, quick-witted, schemer, at a loss, fundamental insecurity, mask, impudence, take seriously, recognition, frustration, channel their energies, fertile, counterfeiter, versatile, go to his head, arrogance, alienates, humour, sociability*

Rooster: *abrasive, aggressive, resolute, shrewd, alert, precise, reserved, neglected, stamina, vitality, contribute, stimulating, perfectionist, tolerance, second-rate*

Dog: *fidelity, humour, steady, trusted, valued, handicapped, conservatism, adjust, defensive, maligned, shoulder to cry on, displays, justified, be relied on, friction, eagerness, mix (socially)*

Pig: *ambitions, benefits, prime concern, shunning, displays, pretence, jollity, caring, industrious, bear evidence, aptitude, carpentry, needlework, put the last touches to, naive, trusting, easy prey, confidence trickster, caring professions, counselling, hospitable, varied*

How to use the activity

Make at least one copy of each text (see below for details of quantities and distribution, according to class size). Make enough copies of the worksheet for each student to have one each.

Begin by discussing horoscopes. Get the students to work out what star sign and year animal they are, if they don't already know:

Aries 21 March – 20 April, Taurus 21 April – 21 May, Gemini 22 May – 21 June, Cancer 22 June – 23 July, Leo 24 July – 23 August, Virgo 24 August – 23 September, Libra 24 September – 23 October, Scorpio 24 October – 22 November, Sagittarius 23 November – 21 December, Capricorn 22 December – 20 January, Aquarius 21 January – 19 February, Pisces 20 February – 20 March

Rat	1936	1948	1960	1972	1984	1996
Ox	1937	1949	1961	1973	1985	1997
Tiger	1938	1950	1962	1974	1986	1998
Hare	1939	1951	1963	1975	1987	1999
Dragon	1940	1952	1964	1976	1988	2000
Snake	1941	1953	1965	1977	1989	2001
Horse	1930	1942	1954	1966	1978	1990
Sheep	1931	1943	1955	1967	1979	1991
Monkey	1932	1944	1956	1968	1980	1992
Rooster	1933	1945	1957	1969	1981	1993
Dog	1934	1946	1958	1970	1982	1994
Pig	1935	1947	1959	1971	1983	1995

Give out the texts. There are twenty-four altogether (twelve Western horoscopes and twelve Chinese horoscopes) and you should ensure that they are all given out. If you have twelve students, give everyone two texts: a Western horoscope and a Chinese horoscope. If you have twenty-four or more students, give everyone one text each. If you have between twelve and twenty-four students, give the faster students two texts and the slower students one text. The activity is not really suitable for fewer than twelve because of the length and density of reading matter. If you do not have enough students in your class, see if you can combine classes with a colleague.

Try to ensure that no one gets the horoscope for their own star sign or year animal. Give them some time to read the texts, asking you for help if necessary.

Give each student a copy of the worksheet.and ask them to complete it. While they are completing the worksheet, circulate and deal with problems and queries.

When they have finished, ask them to stand up and go around the class talking to other students.

The object of the activity is to find the person who can tell them their Western horoscope and the person who can tell them their Chinese horoscope.

You could finish off with a class or group discussion on whether the two analyses were similar or totally different, which was closer to the truth, etc.

Key: Answers to the worksheet will vary.

Follow-up: Students can write a comparison of the two character analyses.

23 Dream merchants

Type of activity
whole class mêlée
retelling a dream and finding the interpretation

Level/Time required
advanced (though dream texts are easier than almanacs)/longer than average

Games material
Dream almanacs A, B, C, D, E
Dreams 1–5

Function practised
narrating past events, predicting the future

Structures
past tenses, *will*, present simple, *if*

Lexical areas
townscapes, landscapes, animals, emotions

Problem vocabulary

Dream almanac A: *denotes, unsettled, locality, acorns, betokens, abundance, omen, prosperity, speedy, recovery, sly, crafty, caution, almonds, relish, undertaking, prosperous, enterprise, speculation, penetrates, scheming, arrow, bats, rival, hardships, accomplished, achieved, overcoming, foe, contradiction, debilitate, residence, bounty, foretells, ardently, acquirement, fortune, advancement, muddy, labour, beware, disaster, indication, pecuniary, fortune, delay*

Dream almanac B: *brambles, injured, overcome, duration, abundance, posterity, sufficiency, affliction, sorrow, contradiction, forerunner, grief, foretell, deceive, impediment, undertakings, prosper, hasty, burdens, disasters, heroism, rid, feasting, rejoicing, portends, snuffed, grazing, cattle, affluence, diligent, industrious, violent, enable, eminent, speedy, misfortune, roughly, suspended, sorrow, prosperity, corn, omen, perennial honeymoon, stumble, temporal, imprudence, ultimate, regain, reputation, favour, honour, desire*

Dream almanac C: *boisterous, trials, echo, proposed, idolize, trade, advancement, rotten, treacherous, abode, gaze, flourish, betokens, contradiction, cautious, procedure, fair, portends, negligence, rivalry, fairy, falcon, envy, injuring, eminence, precipice, bestow, embarrassment, mushroom, evergreen, perennial, advancement, bequeath, partaking, unengaged*

Dream almanac D: *affliction, fawn, deer, inconstancy, fruitfulness, fever, circumstances, fragrant, indication, undertake, bind, bouquet, scattered, sanguine, blasted, denotes, trade, aspire, qualified, applied, assistance, speculating, shares, ruin, vanish, labour, toil, lucrative, virtuous, disposition, industrious, betokens, thwarted, foretells, desolate, fertile, vegetation, implies, favourable, match, harbinger, adorned, speedy, inspecting, fortunate, flourishing, import, ambition, portent, honour, glory, climax*

Dream almanac E: *expectations, savage, overcome, reception, destined, crowned with, virtuous, foretells, denotes, trade, prosperity, flowing, abundance, cattle, crops, quit, commence, on your own account, portends,*

reunion, betokens, stirring, favourable, gaze, ocean, turbid, augurs, accomplishment, devoutly, prognosticates, foreshows, courtship, matrimony, mutual, endearing, parrot, emigrate, cultivate, amass, honour, secure, esteem, reside, populous, flourishing, triumph, portends, rainbow, muddy, unblemished, harassed, unscathed

Dream 1: *steep, brambles, scratched, thorns, orchard, almonds, laden, ladder, surrounded*

Dream 2: *desert, bats, crouched, beaks, mirage, floated, orchards, rocked, fertile, brilliant, inland, dense, parrots*

Dream 3: *towers, bustling, galloping, cornfield*

Dream 4: *candle, leopard, struggle, enormous, growling, snarling, wounded, bleeding, scrambled, rainbow*

Dream 5: *alligator, jaws, snap, eluded, stumbled, tripped, consciousness, almonds*

How to use the activity

Make enough copies of each of the ten texts, Dream almanacs A–E and Dreams 1–5, for one tenth of the students.
Begin by asking the students if they can remember any vivid or interesting dreams they have had. Ask them to tell each other in pairs. Do they have any interpretations of their dream: what did it mean to them? Tell them that they are going to find out some traditional explanations for the symbols in dreams from a book called *Old Moore's Dream Almanack.*
Divide the class in two. Half the class will be dream merchants, and half will be dreamers. Make sure there are at least five people in the merchants group, even if it means the two groups are uneven in size. Divide the merchants group into five sub-groups and give each sub-group a text, Dream almanac A B C D or E. Give each person in the dreamers group a dream 1 2 3 4 or 5, making sure as many different dreams as possible are distributed. Give them some time to read their text and go round helping with problems as they come up.
Then seat each of the five dream merchants groups at desks spaced around the room. Ask the dreamers to stand up. Tell them they are in a market where the dream merchants are selling various interpretations of dreams.
The object of the activity is to go round the five merchants and find out what their dream means.
When all the dreamers have been round and found the meaning of the symbols in their dreams, you can if you like swap roles so the dreamers are now merchants and vice versa. Alternatively you can round the activity off by asking five dreamers to recount their dreams and explain the meaning. This can lead into a group discussion on the interpretation of dreams.

Key: Dream 1 – difficulties and problems in life will be overcome. You will be successful in trade and love, will become rich, travel to a foreign land and marry a foreigner, recover from an illness and reach the height of ambition. Dream 2 – A difficult journey, dangerous. An enemy. These will be overcome and you will have happiness in love and prosperity, marriage and good fortune, although one lover will be unfaithful. You will travel to a foreign country and have two children, a boy and a girl. Dream 3 – You will have enough money to travel and see the world. You will success in trade and love, a happy marriage, money and good children. There will be good news – you will be married soon and life will be a perennial honeymoon. A numerous family! Dream 4 – You will get a pleasant letter soon and hear news which will cause you to leave your job and travel to a foreign lane. You will have difficulties but will overcome them and be happy and prosperous. A change for the better. Dream 5 – You have an enemy and are entering a period of uncertainty but it will end. You will marry a rich foreigner and live in a foreign country. You will be rich, have a long and happy life and be successful.

Follow-up: Students can write an account of a dream they once had. Alternatively, play some gentle music and ask them to close their eyes and 'dream' and write up the dream afterwards.

24 Politically correct

Type of activity
six groups then whole class mêlée
finding out definitions of politically correct terms and filling in speech bubbles in cartoons

Level/Time required
advanced/shorter than average

Games material
Texts: The politically correct dictionary A-F
Cartoon worksheet

Function practised
finding euphemisms

Structures
various, past participle as adjective

Lexical areas
the socially disadvantaged

Problem vocabulary

A: *dentation, canine, cerebrally, inconvenienced, chemically, chronologically, redundancy*

B: *advantaged, logical, incarceration, survivor*

C: *finalization, ethically, disorientated, experientially, enhanced, follicle, horizontally, challenged*

D: *transition, idled, indefinitely, unmet, objectives, inoperative, involuntarily, leisured, undomiciled*

E: *metabolically, motivationally, deficient, outcome, optically, inconvenienced*

F: *sobriety, adjustment, pharmacological, awareness, temporally, terminally, inconvenienced, vertically, challenged*

How to use the activity
Make a copy of the cartoon worksheet for each student. Make enough copies of text A for one sixth of the students to have a copy each, and the same for texts B, C, D, E and F. Give each student a copy of the worksheet and ask them to look at the first cartoon. Explain the idea of 'politically correct' language – language that avoids criticising or making value judgements about people's shortcomings or

deficiencies. Ask the students if they can guess the meaning of some of the following examples, taken from the texts. How would they normally describe someone who is: hair disadvantaged; an incomplete success; optically inconvenienced; in a reduced state of awareness?
Then divide the class into six groups, A, B, C, D, E and F. Give text A to each student in group A, text B to all those in group B and so on. Tell them that the definitions are in muddled order and that their job as a group is to match each politically correct phrase with its definition. Go round and help as necessary. (They may need dictionaries – ordinary ones! – to help with some of the terms.)
When they have finished and correctly matched each phrase with its definition, ask them to look at their cartoon worksheet.
The object of the activity is to fill in the speech bubbles with the appropriate 'translation' in 'correct' language. To do this, they will have to get up and move around the class asking people from other groups to translate words or phrases for them.
Round the activity off by returning everyone to their groups and asking them to compare cartoons.

Key: A fat, false teeth, deaf, dog living in USA, redundancy, stupid, boring, drunk, old; B poor, boring, wrong, fat, liar, antisocial, housewife, housework, housewife; C unfinished, crazy, dishonest, old, bald, bald, fat; D unemployed, failure, unemployed, failure, mistake, unemployed, homeless, worst; E dead, evil, lazy, death, corpse, spendthrift, shoplifeter, blind; F drunk, recession, serial killer, addiction, drunk, late, dead, homeless, short

Worksheet 1 'I'm afraid your canine American is terminally inconvenienced/metabolically different'; 2 'I'm underhoused/involuntarily undomiciled and in an orderly transition between career changes/indefinitely idled/involuntarily leisured.'; 3 'Your little boy is ethically disorientated, cerebrally challenged, motivationally deficient and morally different.'; 4 'vertically and horizontally challenged/differently sized.'; 5 'terminally inconvenienced ... just in a reduced state of awareness/metabolically different/chemically inconvenienced.'; 6 'You're horizontally challenged/differently sized, differently interesting/charm free, follicularly challenged/hair disadvantaged, experientially enhanced/chronologically challenged and an incomplete success/individual with temporarily unmet objectives.'

Follow-up: Each group could design its own cartoon.

A

Botticelli

One member of the group leaves the room and the rest think of a famous person, e.g. Boris Yeltsin. The person is recalled and tries to guess who the group have chosen, by asking questions such as 'Am I a famous female pop star?' The group must then answer with the name of the pop star they think the person means, for example, 'No you're not Madonna.' If they answer correctly, then the guesser must try again, but if they get the name wrong – if for example the guesser was thinking of Tracy Chapman, not Madonna – then they must give the guesser three clues about the identity of the person they have chosen, for example, 'You are alive,' 'You're male,' 'You live in Europe.' The guesser must then restrict his guesses to males living in Europe, for example, 'Am I a famous British footballer who plays for an Italian team?'

B

The Parson's Cat

The players sit in a circle and take turns to play this game. There are two versions, easy and hard. In the easy version the first player begins by saying 'The parson's cat is an *angry* cat,' or some other adjective beginning with A. The next player must continue with an adjective beginning with B, for example, 'The parson's cat is a *beautiful* cat.' The third player must go on with an adjective beginning with C and so on round the group till all the letters of the alphabet have been used. In the hard version, the first player must begin as before with an adjective beginning with A, but this time the second player must also find an adjective beginning with A, for example 'The parson's cat is an *adorable* cat.' and so on round the group until every player has found an adjective beginning with A. Then in the second round, everyone must find an adjective beginning with B, and so on. In this version it is obviously harder for the players who come last to think of adjectives, so it is better to change the order of playing every round so that the player who is last in the first round is not last in every round.

C

Crambo

One member of the group is sent out of the room, while the rest decide on a word, for example *hot*. They then call the person back into the room and give him/her a clue: a word that rhymes with the word they have chosen, for example, *what*. He/she must then try to find the word they have chosen, but may not guess directly. Instead he/she must ask questions such as, 'Is it used for cooking?' to which the group reply, 'No, it's not a *pot*.' Or 'Does it mean many?' to which the group reply, 'No it's not *lot*.' and so on, until he/she asks 'Does it mean warm?' when the group may tell him/her the answer. If he/she asks a question which the group cannot answer because they cannot guess the word he/she means, then he/she has won and they must tell him/her their word.

D

The Adverb Game

One person is sent out of the room, while the others think of an adverb such as *angrily*, *lazily*, *unhappily*, etc. When they have decided on the adverb, the missing person is recalled and has to guess the adverb they have chosen, by asking members of the group to perform actions in the manner of the adverb, for example, 'Rosita, could you walk to the door in the manner of the adverb,' or 'Fahed, could you look out of the window in the manner of the adverb.' The person asked must then perform the action angrily, lazily, unhappily, etc. according to the adverb the group have chosen. When the guesser has seen a few actions he/she can try to guess the adverb. The group can only say 'Yes' or 'No'. If he/she guesses wrong then he/she can ask other people to perform different actions until he/she can guess correctly.

A   A successful author

'I did very badly at school. My headmaster thought I was useless and when I was 14 he said, 'You're never going to be anything but a failure.'

After five years in dead-end jobs, I fell in love with a very nice middle-class student. It was the best thing that could have happened to me. I decided I wanted to do something positive with my life because I wanted to prove to her that what people said about me was wrong. Especially her mother, who had said to me, 'Let's face it, you've failed at everything you've ever done.' So I tried hard with my writing and went to college. My first novel was published while I was at college.

After college I taught during the day in secondary schools and signed up as an evening class student at London University, where I got a degree in sociology and social psychology. I became a senior lecturer at a teacher-training college and was thinking of giving up that job to write full time when I was offered a part-time job at Leeds University. It was really good for my ego – here was a working-class boy who'd left school early, now teaching at the university.

My writing career only took off when I invented a new name and changed my style. Until then I was trying to copy other people and for the first time I discovered my own style.

Up till then I was selling about 3500 copies in hardback of each novel. Then I started on a new book.

My editor rang up and asked what I was working on. I told him I was writing a book in which some Germans disguised as British paratroopers try to kidnap Winston Churchill. He said, 'That's the worst idea I've ever heard. Who's interested in a bunch of Germans trying to get Winston Churchill?' Well 13 million people were interested.

I've never got such pleasure from writing. I don't know what my motivation is – I'm not writing for the money now. I don't need it. I've made about £10 million in the past 10 years. I'm rich and famous, I've been on TV, been to Buckingham Palace, met lots of film stars. But what does it mean? I just wish all the people that have put me down had said, 'I like you. I believe in you. I'm on your side.''

B   A famous actress

'When I left drama school I thought I was wonderful. So I went to New York to look for a job. My problem was that I didn't look Indian enough for the Indian parts and I didn't look Western enough to be cast in Western parts. And I wasn't voluptuous enough to be a film star in India.

I got a job at 10 dollars a week, agreeing to cook and iron for a film director. Every two or three years I'd get a little part in a film. In one play I got the lead role, but it closed after a week. I used to go to auditions where there'd be 200 people, and I'd never get a part. So I would go home totally depressed.

By this time I had three children and one day I happened to read my daughter's school essay on her mother: 'Eight o'clock my mother is asleep, nine o'clock my mother is asleep, 10 o'clock my mother is asleep, 11 o'clock …' I would get up, feed them and then go back to bed. I just couldn't face life. It was even hard to get auditions: no one would look at me because I was the wrong type. No agent would take me on. I thought of giving up but something made me go on and I kept repeating to myself, 'I'm not going to give up'.

There came a time when I would go into an agent's office and just burst into tears. One agent tried to get me to sleep with him and when I said, 'No,' he said that I wouldn't get any work because my nose was too big. Then I met a film director who asked me to act in a film about a troupe of actors travelling around India performing Shakespeare. We made it and I didn't expect anything to happen but suddenly I won the Best Actress Award at the Berlin Film Festival. I thought, 'I've finally done it.' But it led nowhere. That was the biggest disappointment. I had some dreadful part-time jobs – working a telex, modelling … Three or four years passed before I got any acting at all.

My marriage broke up and I remarried. I used to cook and entertain a lot and someone suggested that I do a cookery book. I agreed thinking it would take me three months. It took five years! The cookery book career slowly began to become a success and in the end I was writing for all the best American magazines, and the BBC asked me to do a cookery series and as a result of that I've had much more interesting acting work than ever before.

My two careers have caused me some misery, because I see myself mainly as an actress: I have just had to turn down the biggest part that I have ever been offered in a major Hollywood film because of obligations to a TV cookery series. I cried for two days.

There are some people who will take 'No' for an answer and some people who won't. However, even people like me, who are very determined, sometimes feel so discouraged that they want to say, 'All right, I accept that. Nothing is ever going to happen in my life. Perhaps I should just be a nice mother to my children.' But there is something inside me which keeps eating away at me and is not satisfied.

Some people can accept less than their dreams: I am dissatisfied with a limited kind of success – I need something bigger.''

C A successful footballer

'When I was 18 I went for a trial. The manager, said that he didn't think I would ever be a professional footballer. Then after another trial they told me I wasn't good enough and sent me home. But my dad always encouraged me, he always used to say, 'Don't worry abut it. It might take time but you'll get there'. At school, football was the only thing that I was interested in, so it was very disappointing to be rejected.

I was beginning to get worried; then suddenly two clubs offered me a contract, and I signed with one of them. Two weeks later I was playing in their first team.

Two years later a Canadian team offered me a contract. Anyway, I married my fiancée and we both flew to Vancouver – it was our first flight.

While I was there, a top British team came over and played against us. I played very well and their manager paid to have me on loan for five months. He paid £250,000 and agreed to pay £250,000 if he decided to keep me. If he didn't keep me on he would get the £250,000 back.

I was 23 and United was my dream. But I had to miss the first five weeks because I was in Vancouver, and by the time I got to Britain, United was winning every game and the manager was reluctant to change a winning side.

Eventually I had a chance to play but for some reason we didn't play our best. I was taken off and another player brought on. As I walked off I thought, 'That's it. I've messed that up!'

That was very unlucky but I still felt that I was good enough to make it. I wanted to get my last year in Canada over quickly and return to England. Then I was picked for England and established myself as an international. I now had the confidence to pick my club.

I've got a wonderful wife and obviously I can afford to buy her things I couldn't before. My mother was lucky if she got £5 for her birthday; now I can buy her a microwave.

I still have trouble believing that my picture is in the paper. My wife says I'm like a little child amazed by it all – but I still can't believe that it's happened to me.

D A successful pop singer

People always tell you that you're too old to do what you want. I was 26 when I wanted to be a singer, and they said that was too old. At the advanced age of 22 I went to art college where everybody else was 18. People said it was about time I settled down and did something sensible. But I wanted to try out different things. In my second year at college I joined a local band, found I really liked it and left the college.

We did very well for a couple of years but two years later the group disbanded and I got together with a mate to write songs. We got a keyboard and a recording system and spent all our income sending cassettes to record companies, who rejected all of them …. One letter said, 'Dear Tape Maker' and there was a list of comments with little boxes for them to tick. For us they ticked 'Don't give up your job'.

You have your heart in your mouth when you're Little Miss Nobody

sending off tapes. You think at the time that the setbacks are going to destroy you but they don't – they make you more determined.

My father once said to me, 'You're nearly 30. How long do you think you can go on being on the dole and living in poverty?' Mother turned to me and said, 'Promise me that you won't ever give up.' I've been so short of money that I've had no money to put in the gas meter and I've sat in a sleeping bag with a hot-water bottle watching television. The three of us (me, my partner and the dog) lived on £15 a week. It was terrible. But at my lowest point – and I've had some extremely low ones – I would never have dreamt of giving up because life without music is not worth living.

Then one record company said, 'The girl's voice isn't bad. What does she look like?' I rushed round getting a group together and we made two songs for the audition. The director of the

company said, 'Wonderful. Let's talk'. When he left we yelled and jumped up and down with excitement. This was our breakthrough. A proper London record company was interested in us.

Our first record was released and was a disaster. I was shocked because I knew it was a really good pop song. Then it was released in the US and got to number four. This meant it was re-released in England, and went to number four here too. So all the people who didn't like it at first suddenly started to like it. But I don't feel hurt: I think it's quite amusing.

I'm prepared to take risks. I'm prepared to fail but want all the success when I've made the right decision.

Our second record did nothing, then the third was number one for five weeks.

So perhaps I wasn't too old after all.

E A successful cartoonist

'These days people say to me, 'Your work's everywhere. It's so commercial. You've sold out.' That's rubbish. I've been working in the same way for years, and for years it was rejected.

When things changed it had nothing to do with me. I didn't change. What changed was the time, the place and the climate of opinion.

When I left art school I soon decided to become a cartoonist. I thought that my work was good and funny but people just weren't interested. I was getting desperate because I knew that I was doing something good, but I was incredibly poor and needed a way of making an income out of it.

I got a job teaching part-time in a school in north London. It was hell on earth going into a room of 30 girls armed with knives. And all the time I went round trying to sell my work to people who fell asleep as they looked at it.

At one time I showed my work to a postcard publisher. He said, 'There's no commercial potential here. You should try this sort of thing.' And he showed me a few examples of cartoons he liked. That really infuriated me.

The worst experience I had was with a gallery owner in New York. I had an introduction from a famous artist but she hardly looked at my work. She spent most of the time looking out of the window. At the end she said, 'Well, thank you, for your time,' and I said 'Thank you' and staggered out on to the street and one of my teeth fell out. It was not a good day.

Then one day an Australian saw my work and offered me an exhibition in Australia. So I put my work in a suitcase, went to the airport and missed the plane. And that was one of the best things that ever happened to me. The following day a London exhibitions organiser phoned me and said, 'We'd like to show you. Have you got any work available?' I said I had a suitcase full.

And that was it. The show was reviewed everywhere; we made postcards that sold hundreds of thousands of copies. Several publishers phoned up with offers of books. It was exactly the same work that I had been doing for years – I hadn't changed at all. I just thought: 'Where were all of you 10 years ago?'

I have no respect for people's opinion of my work. One day everyone says, 'This is terrible, go away,' and a few years later they're saying, 'You're a genius.' It's the same work and I don't care what they think of it. The only thing that is important is that I'm happy with it. There's nothing people can say to change what I produce. It didn't happen when I was a failure and it's not going to happen now I'm a success.'

F A successful actor

'In the theatre you're not supposed to want success – you have to pretend that you never wanted it. But rejection is especially hard for an actor, because if you're rejected it's your body, the way you sound, the way you look that is being rejected. It's a very personal rejection and very difficult to cope with.

As a child I lived in South Africa and my parents decided that I should go to Britain to study acting. We had found out which was the best drama school and decided that that was where I would go. They even rented a flat for me.

When I was 19 I arrived in England from South Africa and a week later I had an audition at the school. It was a frightening but short experience which lasted about 10 minutes. The group of us that had auditioned had to wait in a small room and the registrar put her head round the corner and said, 'None of you today.' I couldn't believe that I'd travelled half-way across the world just to get a rejection. I went back to the hotel convinced that there would be a message for me saying 'There's been a mistake we didn't mean you.' But they did.

Then I went for an audition at another school. That school didn't let me know immediately; they sent me a letter, which said something like, 'Not only have you failed to get in, not only do we not want you to try again but we recommend that you think of a different career.'

Without my parents' encouragement I would have given up. Eventually I got into another school, but when I left the principal said some things that I found very depressing. He told me that I wasn't going to be a success until my thirties.

I remember being deeply disappointed when I didn't get a part in a play in London's West End. It was a part that I thought especially was made for me.

One of the things that my therapist has taught me was that it is very important to be able to evaluate your own work. It's a very hard thing to do because you've got the director, fellow actors, the audience and the critics all giving their own opinions.

Last year I suddenly realised that I had become part of the British theatre establishment. I was asked to play in a cabaret to celebrate Laurence Olivier's (Britain's most famous actor) 80th birthday. It was the most scaring night of my life. I thought of my grandfather, who was a barely literate Lithuanian peddler, and I suddenly saw how far I had come.'

Reading Games, © Jill Hadfield and Charles Hadfield 1995

The interviewer asked these questions. How did your character reply?

1 When did you first start wanting to do what you're doing now?

2 Did you always want to do it, or was there another career that tempted you?

3 How did you make a start in your career?

4 Things were difficult for you at the beginning, weren't they? Who turned you down? For what reasons?

5 How did you have the strength to keep going?

6 Did you get much encouragement from your family or friends?

7 When did your lucky break come?

8 How 'successful' would you say you are now?

9 Have you learnt any lessons from your experience?

A THE CRIMES THAT WERE EASIEST TO DETECT

Any act of genius is marked by a dazzling simplicity. There is about it a logic and inevitability that is deeply satisfying. The following crimes were detected almost immediately after they had been committed.

In 1972 Mr J Egan from London stole a barge on the River Thames and was very soon caught. There was a dock strike on and his was the only craft moving that day.

Mr J Ealey committed a burglary in Detroit in 1968 and left his dog at the scene of the crime. The police soon arrived and shouted 'Home boy'. They then followed the dog back to the burglar's house. And arrived only seconds after he did.

In May 1976 Vernon Drinkwater and Raymond Heap of Blackburn were accused of stealing a car while trying to sell it to its original owner.

 ## B THE LEAST WELL-PLANNED ROBBERY

Three thieves at Billericay in Essex gave hours of thought in 1971 to raiding the Post Office in Mountnessing Road.

Among the details which they discovered were the times at which there was most cash and least security guard on the premises. They also invested in masks, guns and a getaway car.

At a pre-arranged time, the Mountnessing gang sped through Billericay and screeched to a halt outside the post office.

It was only when they jumped out of the car and ran towards the building that they discovered the one detail which they had omitted to check.

The Post Office had been closed for twelve years.

 ## C THE LEAST PROFITABLE ROBBERY

Intending to steal cash from a supermarket in 1977, a Southampton thief employed a unique tactic to divert the till girl's attention. His method was to collect a trolley full of goods, arrive at her till and put down £10 by way of payment. She would then take the money and open the till, upon which he would snatch the contents.

He arrived at the cash desk and put down the £10. She took it and opened the till; but there was only £4.37 in it.

Undeterred, the Southampton thief snatched that and made his getaway, having lost £5.63 on the raid.

The till girl was considerably uncertain what to do for the best. She screamed briefly until calmed by her friend Betty.

 ## D THE MOST UNSUCCESSFUL PRISON ESCAPE

After weeks of extremely careful planning, seventy-five convicts completely failed to escape from Saltillo Prison in Northern Mexico. In November 1975 they had started digging a secret tunnel designed to bring them up at the other side of the prison wall.

On 18 April 1976, guided by pure genius, their tunnel came up in the nearby courtroom in which many of them had been sentenced. The surprised judges returned all 75 to jail.

 ## E THE WORST BANK ROBBERS

In August 1975 three men were on their way in to rob the Royal Bank of Scotland at Rothesay, when they got stuck in the revolving doors. They had to be helped free by the staff and, after thanking everyone, sheepishly left the building.

A few minutes later they returned and announced their intention of robbing the bank, but none of the staff believed them. When, at first, they demanded £5,000, the head cashier laughed at them, convinced that it was a practical joke.

Considerably disheartened by this, the gang leader reduced his demand first to £500, then to £50 and ultimately to 50 pence. By this stage the cashier could barely control herself for laughter.

Then one of the men jumped over the counter and fell awkwardly on the floor, clutching at his ankle. The other two made their getaway, but got trapped in the revolving doors for a second time, desperately pushing the wrong way.

Reading Games, © Jill Hadfield and Charles Hadfield 1995

F THE MOST UNSUCCESSFUL ATTEMPT TO WORK THROUGH A LUNCH HOUR

Mr Stanley Hird surely set a record in June 1978 when trying to catch up on some paperwork. At one o'clock his carpet factory outside Bradford was deserted and he settled down for an uninterrupted hour. At ten past one a cow fell through the roof. The cow had clambered on to the roof from the adjoining field. For thirty seconds they stared at each other and then the cow, who had also been planning a quiet lunch hour, lowered her head and charged. This continued for some minutes, during which time Mr Hird retreated steadily towards the door as the cow scattered stacks of wool. Eventually the heifer, whose name was Rosie, stopped to chew a green carpet and Mr Hird escaped into the corridor. Here he met a farmer who inquired if he had seen a heifer. Police, firemen and an elaborate set of pulleys were needed to extract the animal.

G THE LEAST SUCCESSFUL ATTEMPT TO MEET A RELATIVE AT AN AIRPORT

In 1975 Mrs Josephine Williams and her family went to meet a long-lost brother at Heathrow Airport. They took home a complete stranger.

Greatly relaxed by in-flight drinking facilities, the traveller wandered into the airport lounge to be smothered by the kisses of Mrs Williams and her sisters. 'Gee, this is great,' he kept saying, all the while cuddling Mrs Williams in a manner which she later described as 'not like a brother'.

His enthusiasm for British hospitality was modified, however, when Mr Williams shook his hand firmly and ushered him to a parked car.

They first suspected that something was amiss when their relative tried to jump out of the car while travelling at speed up the motorway.

When told that he was being taken to a family reunion in Coventry, he replied, 'Take my money. Here's my wallet. Take it and let me go.'

Slumped miserably in the front seat, he added, 'This is the first time I have been to England and I am being kidnapped.''

I thought from the beginning he wasn't my brother,' Mrs Williams said later, 'but my sisters wouldn't listen. They said I was only twelve when he left for America and wouldn't remember.'

H THE LEAST SUCCESSFUL ANIMAL RESCUE

The firemen's strike of 1978 made possible one of the great animal rescue attempts of all time. Valiantly, the British Army had taken over emergency firefighting and on 14 January they were called out by an elderly lady in South London to retrieve her cat which had become trapped up a tree. They arrived with impressive haste and soon discharged their duty. So grateful was the lady that she invited them all in for tea. Driving off later, with fond farewells completed, they ran over the cat and killed it.

I THE LEAST SUCCESSFUL BANK ROBBER

Not wishing to attract attention to himself, a bank robber in 1969 at Portland, Oregon, wrote all his instructions on a piece of paper rather than shout.

'This is a hold-up and I've got a gun,' he wrote and then held the paper up for the cashier to read.

The bemused bank official waited while he wrote out, 'Put all the money in a paper bag.'

This message was pushed through the grille. The cashier read it and then wrote on the bottom, 'I don't have a paper bag,' and passed it back.

The robber fled.

J THE WORST TOURIST

The least successful tourist on record is Mr Nicholas Scotti of San Francisco. In 1977 he flew from America to his native Italy to visit relatives.

En route the plane made a one-hour fuel stop at Kennedy Airport. Thinking that he had arrived, Mr Scotti got out and spent two days in New York believing he was in Rome.

When his nephews were not there to meet him, Mr Scotti assumed they had been delayed in the heavy Roman traffic mentioned in their letters. While tracking down their address, the great traveller could not help noticing that modernisation had brushed aside most, if not all, of the ancient city's landmarks.

He also noticed that many people spoke English with a distinct American accent. However, he just assumed that Americans got everywhere. Furthermore, he assumed it was for their benefit that so many street signs were written in English.

Mr Scotti spoke very little English himself and next asked a policeman (in Italian) the way to the bus depot. As chance would have it, the policeman came from Naples and replied fluently in the same tongue.

After twelve hours travelling round on a bus, the driver handed him over to a second policeman. There followed a brief argument in which Mr Scotti expressed amazement at the Rome police force employing someone who did not speak his own language.

Scotti's brilliance is seen in the fact that even when told he was in New York, he refused to believe it

To get him on a plane back to San Francisco, he was raced to the airport in a police car with sirens screaming. 'See,' said Scotti to his interpreter, 'I know I'm in Italy. That's how they drive.'

Reading Games, © Jill Hadfield and Charles Hadfield 1995

How many of the following questions can you answer? Answer as many as possible and then share information to complete the questionnaire.

1 Why was the prison escape unsuccessful?

2 Why was Mr Egan caught when he stole a barge?

3 Why was the Post Office robbery unsuccessful?

4 Why did the supermarket thief lose money?

5 What happened to the robbers at the Bank of Scotland?

6 What interrupted Mr Hird's lunch hour?

7 What mistake did Mrs Williams make at the airport?

8 What happened to the cat?

9 What did the cashier write on the piece of paper?

10 Why did Mr Scotti think he was in Rome? Where was he?

How many of the following questions can you answer? Answer as many as possible and then share information to complete the questionnaire.

1 Why was the prison escape unsuccessful?

2 Why was Mr Egan caught when he stole a barge?

3 Why was the Post Office robbery unsuccessful?

4 Why did the supermarket thief lose money?

5 What happened to the robbers at the Bank of Scotland?

6 What interrupted Mr Hird's lunch hour?

7 What mistake did Mrs Williams make at the airport?

8 What happened to the cat?

9 What did the cashier write on the piece of paper?

10 Why did Mr Scotti think he was in Rome? Where was he?

1

A vicar called on an old lady who was one of his parishioners and was fascinated by her talking parrot. But he saw that the bird had a blue ribbon tied to each leg and asked the lady why.

'If I pull the ribbon on his right leg,' she said, 'he sings me a happy hymn – Onward Christian Soldiers – but if I am feeling sad, I pull the ribbon on his left leg and he sings a sad hymn – Abide With Me.'

'Wonderful,' said the vicar. 'And what if you pull both ribbons at once?'

2

A friend of mine was travelling by train and opposite him sat a gentleman reading *The Times*. Every so often he took a sheet of the newspaper, crumpled it up, opened the window, threw it out and shut the window.

After he had done this a few times my friend said, 'Excuse me, but may I ask why you are doing that?'

'Oh yes,' he replied, 'it keeps the elephants away.'

'But,' my friend said, 'there aren't any elephants here.'

3

A man was out for a walk in the town and met a penguin, which started to follow him. Now knowing what to do with it, he took it to the nearest police station and asked for advice.

'Take it to the Zoo,' they advised.

Next day one of the policemen met the man in the street, still followed by the penguin.

'What are you doing with that penguin?' he said. 'I thought you were going to take it to the Zoo.'

The two mice heard a cat approaching their mousehole. 'Miaow ... Miaow ... Miaaoow ...' they heard first. Then 'Woof ... Woof ... Woof ...' the sound of an angry dog, followed by silence.

Cautiously the two mice crept out of their hole – and the cat jumped on them, saying as he ate them up:

A lady was carrying out a survey of drinking habits. She rang the bell of a house and an army colonel answered.

She explained: 'I am doing a survey into people's drinking habits. Would you mind giving me some information about yours?'

'Not at all,' replied the colonel. 'In fact I haven't had a drink since 1945.'

'Congratulations!' said the lady, 'that is quite an amazing achievement.'

A very unpleasant man went to stay with his friend. After dinner his friend said, 'Would you like a coffee?'

'No – tea,' he replied.

Later his friend asked him, 'Would you like a whisky?'

'No – brandy,' he replied.

Next morning his friend asked, 'Would you like a cup of tea with your breakfast?'

'No – coffee,' he replied.

His friend asked, 'Would you like your eggs scrambled or fried?'

'One fried, one scrambled,' he replied.

After breakfast his friend asked, 'Did you enjoy your breakfast?'

7

A man was lonely and bought a canary thinking it would talk to him.

Disappointed by the bird's lack of conversation, he complained to the pet shop owner, who sold him a mirror, and when this failed to make the canary talk, suggested some cuttle-fish wedged between the bars.

This didn't work and the man returned daily to the shop where he was advised in turn to buy a swing, and then a ladder, and finally a bell to give the little bird a purpose in life.

'You will find,' said the pet shop owner, 'once he has had a swing, sharpened his beak on the cuttle-fish, climbed the ladder and rung the bell, he will start talking.'

A week later the man returned triumphant.

'It worked,' he said. 'He looked in the mirror, swung on the swing, climbed the ladder, rang the bell and then fell backwards on to the floor of the cage with his feet in the air.'

'Did he say anything?'

8

A man walked into the doctor's surgery and bumped into a very young and pretty girl coming out, but she was crying bitterly.

'Come on,' he said, 'it can't be that bad.'

She said, 'Oh, but it is, the doctor's just told me I'm pregnant.

The man turned to the doctor and asked

'Is it true?'

The doctor said,

9

A man had just finished his lunch in a restaurant and the waitress asked if he would take coffee.

'Yes, please,' he replied.

The waitress went off but quickly returned and asked, 'With or without cream, sir?'

'Without,' he replied.

After a long wait the waitress returned, rather anxious, and said apologetically,

10

All good stories, should be short and to the point. This was well known to at least one small boy who was asked to write a story in class containing elements of Romance, Royalty, Mystery and Religion, and completed the task in thirty seconds.

When asked by the teacher, he read out,

11

A former President of the United States was holding a dinner at the White House. Among the guests was a Red Indian Chief dressed in full costume.

The President seated his Lady next to the Red Indian Chief, to make him feel comfortable and also because the Chief held 51% of a big oil company.

When the dinner started and soup was served, the President's wife smiled at the Chief and said, 'You like-um soupee?'

The Chief nodded his head.

When the second course was served up she said, 'You like-um turkey?'

Again the Chief smiled and nodded. This went on through every course.

After coffee, the Chief had to make a speech. He stood up and gave a brilliant speech in faultless English.

He sat down to deafening applause, and turning to the President's wife, he said,

12

Two Belgians and two Dutchmen travelled regularly to work on the same train.

After a while the Dutchmen saw that the two Belgians only had one ticket between them and asked how they managed to achieve this. They explained that when they hear the conductor approaching from the other end of the carriage, the two of them left their seats, went into the toilet and locked the door. When the conductor knocked on the toilet door saying, 'Tickets please', they pushed one ticket under the door. It was then stamped and pushed back under the door again.

The Dutchmen thought this was a very good idea and the following morning bought one ticket between them. When they got to their carriage there was only one Belgian. They told him what they had done and asked the Belgian if he had a ticket as he was travelling on his own.

He said he did not have a ticket at all and when they asked how he proposed to manage to travel free of charge, he told them they would have to wait and see until the conductor arrived, but he had no doubt that he would manage it without difficulty.

As soon as they heard the conductor coming the two Dutchmen immediately went to the toilet and locked the door.

Reading Games, © Jill Hadfield and Charles Hadfield 1995

13

A small and weedy man arrived at a lumberjack camp in the northern forests of Canada. All the men working at the camp were at least six feet tall, and simply couldn't believe that the new arrival was a lumberjack. They gave him a very small axe and took him to a small tree. The man chopped the tree down with one blow.

The big lumberjacks immediately decided to teach him a lesson. They gave him one of the largest and heaviest axes that they could find and took him to a particularly tall and thick tree.

'Go on, cut this down,' they said.

'All right,' he replied.

Within a very few minutes the new arrival had sent the big tree crashing down.

'Amazing,' said the lumberjacks, 'but how on earth is it that someone as small and thin as you can cut trees so well? Where do you come from?'

'The Sahara,' he replied.

'But there are no trees in the Sahara,' said one of the lumberjacks.

14

A doctor, an architect and a politician argued whose was the oldest profession.

'Obviously, the medical profession is the oldest,' said the doctor, 'because the first doctor was the one who took the rib out of Adam to create Eve.'

The architect disagreed.

'God was the first architect. He created order out of chaos, so mine must be the oldest profession.'

15

A very successful young tycoon lost his business flair and was so worried he went to see his doctor.

His doctor could find nothing wrong with him but suggested that he should see a brain specialist.

He did this and was told that his brain was prematurely old and worn out but with modern brain transplant surgery he could be given a new one.

He asked abut the cost, and the reply was that it depended on what type of brain he wanted – for example, he could have a legal brain for £10,000, or a doctor's brain for £20,000 or an Army officer's brain for £40,000.

'That's ridiculous! An officer's brain can't cost twice as much as a doctor's!'

'Then I fall off my perch, you silly old fool,' said the parrot.

'Of course not,' he replied. 'That proves it works!'

'Oh,' replied the man. 'That was yesterday. Today we are going to the pictures.'

'I always knew it would be useful to have a second language.'

'I know,' replied the colonel, looking at his watch. 'It is already 20.00 hours.'

'No,' he replied. 'You scrambled the wrong egg.'

'Yes, just before he died he said, "Did no one tell you about bird seed?".'

'No, but it's cured her hiccups.'

'I'm sorry sir. There is no more cream. Will you have it without milk?'

'God,' said the duchess, 'I'm pregnant. Who done it?'

'You like-um speechy?'

A few moments later the Belgian followed them down the corridor and knocked on the toilet door saying, 'Tickets please'. One Dutch ticket appeared under the door.

'Not any more,' replied the new arrival.

'Ah!' said the politician, 'but it was the first politician who created the chaos.'

'Oh, yes,' was the reply. 'You see, it's as good as new; it has never been used.'

A Rabbi

It was a huge heart made of chocolate which opened up and had chocolate creams inside, and I knew exactly who it was from. I was 13 and he was 25 and my first great love. He was a family friend, and he always had glamorous girlfriends, but he was wonderful and I adored him. I was terribly upset when he married a few years later, because he didn't wait for me, but we have been friends all our lives. I never dreamed of sending *him* one; he was too far above me and out of reach.

B Pin up/singer

I've still kept my first card. I was 11 and it was from a boy in my class who drew a picture of himself and me in a big red heart. He was the only blond boy in class so I knew from the picture that it was from him. I told my best friend, who promptly told everybody else, and he got teased by everyone. But we went swimming together that weekend and became good friends. At 13 I sent my Dad a joke one. It said, 'To Pat, you don't know who I am – I think you're dishy.' I put perfume and a big lipstick kiss on it. He believed it and showed it to Mum to make her jealous but she knew that I'd sent it. Last year he was still boasting to his friends about it so I told him the truth; he was really annoyed.

C News presenter

My first Valentine was unforgettable. It was a homemade card with a poem inside. 'Roses are red, Violets are blue, When I grow up, I want to marry you.' I was seven, and had a crush on a handsome boy in my class. I thought it must be from him and excitedly checked his handwriting. I discovered instead that it was from a boy with spots whose nickname was 'Smelly' because his mother gave him meat and onion sandwiches for lunch. I was terribly disappointed.

D Sportswoman

The most surprising one came from a man I worked with. I thought of him just as a friend but then this romantic card with a red silk rose arrived and inside it was a message asking me to propose to him. I only send them to people who are depressed. When I was 12 I sent one to a young boy in my class whom everybody ignored. I signed my name so that he knew he had a friend, and he was very happy. Ever since, I have sent them to boys who aren't the best lookers or who need cheering up.

E Writer

I sent one to myself when I was 13 because I knew no one was interested in me and I wouldn't get one. So I bought it, wrote it and posted it, and when it arrived I took it to school and pretended I had an admirer to save feeling humiliated. The first I really received was from a man in the factory near the office where I worked when I was 16. He could see me sitting by the office window and kept phoning up saying 'Hello, darling'. The card said 'From the factory opposite'. I never did discover who he was. It was a bit frightening, but thrilling. I was working out people's income tax at the time.

F Novelist 1

In my school, founded by idealistic socialists, it was the custom for each child in the class to send a Valentine to every other child. For this purpose we made our own very cheap cards. One 14 February, however, I received a very different sort of Valentine: garlanded with roses and forget-me-nots and trimmed with paper lace. I never found out who sent it, but I dreamed over it for years.

G Presenter

I was hideously ugly when I was at school – as I am now! – and none of the boys liked me. When we were all about seven everyone got Valentines but me, so I made one to send myself. The only trouble was, the cruellest girl in the class saw me so she made sure that everyone knew I'd done it myself and had them all laughing at me. When eventually I did get one, from an Australian boy called Bill, it was a big event in my life. He was so romantic he even waded into a pond in his shoes and socks to get me tadpoles.

H Novelist 2

When I was 14 I sent cards to all the boys I knew. I drew them all myself and they said things like 'Love and Kisses from – Ha Ha Ha'. It really puzzled people. No one guessed except one boy who said, 'That was you, wasn't it?' That was when I learnt that I was a marvellous liar. I don't remember the first one I got: I was much less interested in love than in telling lies!

I Politician

Valentine's Day was really important at school. It didn't matter who they were from, just how many you received. At 12 I got one from a boy I was madly in love with. It was anonymous but I recognised his handwriting and kept it on my dressing table for ages. I once sent a pretend one to my father from a woman called Frou-Frou. His secretary opened it, which was what I had meant to happen, and it caused a bit of fun.

J Scriptwriter

The one I remember best came when I was $16\frac{1}{2}$. There was a knock at the door, and I opened it and saw a taxi leaving. Left on the doorstep was a doll's house, with a note by the bell, saying 'press'. I did, and the windows lit up, a figure came out of the door carrying a red heart, and a tune played 'I'll be loving you'. It was absolutely wonderful. The house even had curtains and a cat at the window. I knew it was from my boyfriend because he was the only person who could have made such an incredible thing. It did the trick! At 17 I married him!

Answer as many questions as you can and then ask other students for help.

1 What was inside the dolls' house?

What tune did it play?

Does she still know the boy who gave her this present?

2 Two people sent Valentines to their fathers. How did they sign them? Who opened them?

3 An Australian boy called Bill sent her her first Valentine. What else did he do for her?

4 How many people sent Valentines to themselves?

5 How many people had to send Valentines to every other child in the class?

6 She got a huge chocolate heart when she was 12. Who was it from?

7 A Valentine arrived for her which said, 'Roses are red, violets are blue, When I grow up, I want to marry you.' How old was she?

Who did she think it was from? Who was it really from?

8 What did the message say that came with the red silk rose?

A

Well I've only been in India two days and already the adventure's started! It took hours to get through customs and immigration, and when I finally got on the bus I realized I'd arrived on the wrong day. There's a curfew on because of anti-government riots, and I only just managed to find a hotel before the six o'clock evening curfew. Yesterday I was nearly shot by police who were trying to control a demonstration , the banks are all closed and I don't know how long I'll be stuck here. With any luck I'll catch a bus to Nepal on Saturday, so you could try sending a letter to American Express in Kathmandu. I hope to be there until the end of April.

Bye for now,   John

B

I made it! A hellish journey from Delhi, seventy people on a bus designed for thirty, with all their luggage. Anyway K is great, I've found a great little hotel in the wing of an old Maharajah's palace, with Buddhas all over the garden and wonderful chocolate cake of all things! This is a bit better than the place I stayed in last week – Kathmandhu jail! I was arrested for smuggling - a case of mistaken identity - luckily the British Consul here was able to get me freed but I won't be able to leave Nepal until the case is heard next month. I want to go trekking in the Himalaya. I'll tell you about that later.

John

C

This is the view from the campground near Namche Bazaar, where we trekked to last month . Everest is another twenty miles or so (a week's walk). In the house to the left of the temple, we were shown a yeti's head, and all the sherpas were talking about yetis. Well that night, I was woken by a scuffling and heavy breathing outside the tent. I thought, 'thieves!' and grabbed my torch. When I stuck my head out of the tent, there was a big brown hairy creature running off on all fours, and it had stolen my rucksack full of tins of food and drink. I woke the others up and they were sure it was a yeti. The trial was okay and I can leave Nepal tomorrow. Probably send you a card from Calcutta.

Regards,   John

Reading Games, © Jill Hadfield and Charles Hadfield 1995

D

Calcutta! What a city. I've never seen anything like it. I can't begin to describe it, just people people everywhere, and all of them so poor I feel ashamed. Somehow it puts things in perspective – I was mugged last week, and I've lost everything, including my passport, traveller's cheques, all my film, my camera. But when I think how lucky I am, compared to the people living on the pavements here, I feel really lucky to be alive.

It'll take another few days to get a new passport, and then I hope to go to Burma. Plane for Rangoon every Tuesday and Thursday.

Will write soon,   *John*

E

This is the most beautiful country I've ever been to, despite the politics. Army are everywhere, but the people are friendly and smile and the food is delicious. Before coming to Mandalay I spent three days at Pagan where there are hundreds of old ruined temples, along by the Irrawaddy river... and I'm lucky to be alive I tell you. I went swimming with some friends, and suddenly there was a crocodile coming towards us. If I'd been a little further out, I wouldn't be writing you this card!! I hope Thailand is a bit safer!
Yours,   *John*

F

Chiang Mai is a lovely town, I could easily stop here and not come home. The hills around are full of 'hill tribe' people in different ethnic costumes, all with their own customs, dances, and languages. We went for a four day trek, sleeping in the villages, which sounds idyllic but in fact we were very lucky not to get kidnapped!! There are a lot of bandits, involved with opium smuggling in and out of Burma, and the Burmese side is in a state of civil war. Last month some French tourists were kidnapped, and some Americans were murdered only a few weeks ago. We were having lunch by a river when shooting started on the other bank, and suddenly we were surrounded by a dozen or so guerillas in jungle camouflage. Luckily our guide spoke their language, and even better we weren't armed so the guerillas could see we were only tourists. We gave them our cameras and money, and they helped themselves to all the food, but apart from that we are lucky to be alive! Next stop Hong Kong.

   John

G

Back in civilization. You can't imagine how good it felt to have a proper hot bath and buy some new clothes, after so long wandering around Asia. Coffee! Orange juice! Hamburgers! Hong Kong is so strange, like England (roadsigns, buses, shops) but with super food and the noise and bustle of China. I haven't got time, unfortunately, to go north into the People's Republic, that will have to wait till my next trip! Next stop Bali (my plane's tomorrow) – a five-day stopover and then on to Sydney.

Regards, John

H

Tropical Paradise – well almost. I don't think they have hooded cobras in heaven. Or do they? I was in the shower at our guesthouse, and was just drying myself off when I saw something move near the door. I put my glasses on, and just froze. A huge black cobra was waiting in the doorway, staring at me. I really did not know what on earth to do, whether to scream for help or not. I stood there, and the snake waited and waited. It's so hot here, but my blood froze. Amazing stroke of luck, and I'll never forget this, a cat came up ever so quietly behind the snake, pounced and grabbed it behind the neck. Result? One dead cobra, one proud cat, and one very shaken John! I told the landlord, and he said 'Cobra? Yes, he bad one, but never mind, bathroom clean if snake live in there.' Hope my next stop is safer. Do kangaroos bite?

Yours, John

I

Home at last – well nearly. I'll be on BA904 Sydney-Heathrow arriving London Heathrow at 0840 on Tuesday. It'd be great if you could meet me, but bring a wheelchair! I had such a great time in Bali, and then flew on to Sydney. I forgot which way the traffic went, and crossing the road I was literally knocked down by a bus! Both my legs broken, and some broken ribs, I got to the hospital in an ambulance, to find someone had stolen my bag while I was lying in the street. So, no passport, no money left, just a loan of £100 and the airfare from the British High Commission.

See you next week.
Yours in plaster, John

Mark on the map the section of his journey (A–I) that John describes in his postcard.
Then mark the appropriate symbol on the map.

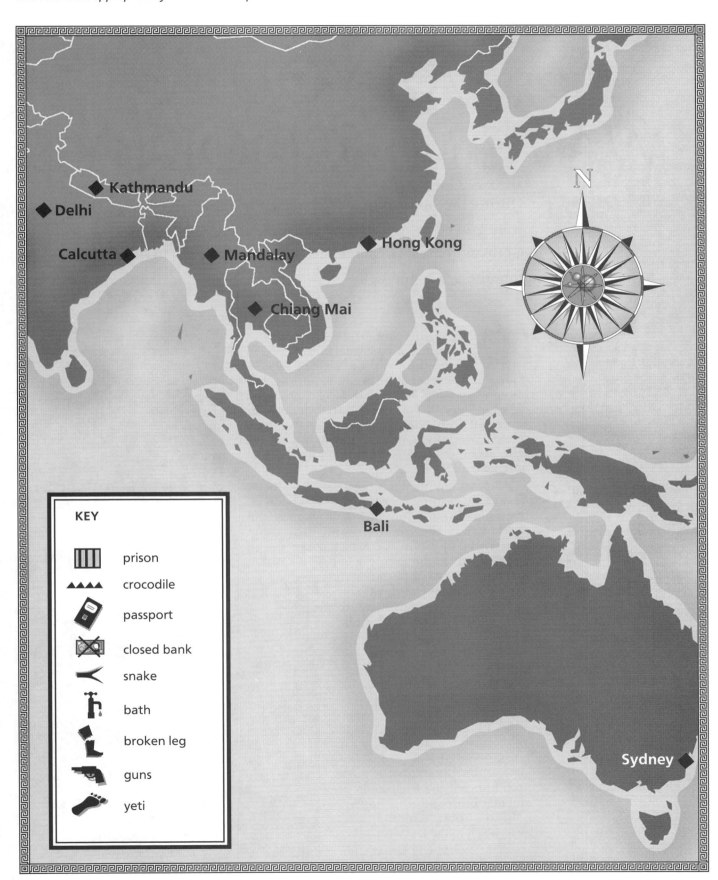

KEY

|||| prison

▲▲▲▲ crocodile

passport

closed bank

snake

bath

broken leg

guns

yeti

Kathmandu
Delhi
Calcutta
Mandalay
Chiang Mai
Hong Kong
Bali
Sydney

N

Reading Games, © Jill Hadfield and Charles Hadfield 1995

WISH ME LUCK AS YOU WAVE ME GOODBYE

During the summer of 1939, thousands of British children were moved from urban homes to escape the threat of German bombs. For some, the new rural life was idyllic; for others, a living hell.

'I thought it was an outing to the seaside. I looked out of the window and saw my mother crying. I said to my brother, "What is mummy crying for?" '

'I went on to enjoy some halycon days over the next six years, growing up on a 200-acre farm in Norfolk.'

The evacuation of thousands and thousands of youngsters from London when the war broke out was a masterpiece of organisation. It was also an operation that was to have a profound effect in later life on the children, who were uprooted from their homes and, with their Mickey Mouse gas masks, dispatched to live with strangers in what often amounted to a 'foreign land'.

I know how they felt because I was one of them, a six-year-old cockney more familiar with the smells and sounds of Billingsgate fish market than with manure and bird song. Certainly I came in for my share of rough treatment from the family who first took me in, but I went on to enjoy some halycon days over the next six years, growing up on a 200–acre farm in Norfolk, which changed me from young 'city slicker' into the country–lover I am to this day.

The brief definition of 'evacuee' in the 'Everyday English Dictionary' – 'a person transferred from a vulnerable to a safe area on account of air raids' – may be accurate as a general description, but it gives no inkling of the thousands of stories, both sad and happy, behind that momentous evacuation in the last war.

MICHAEL CAINE

A

At first everyone was very nice and then the woman that had taken us there left and we sat down to eat. The woman said, 'Here's your meal,' and she gave us a tin of pilchards between the two of us, and some bread and water. Now we'd been in this rich woman's house so we said, 'Where's the butter?' And we suddenly got a wallop round the head. From then on it started...not the husband he was never there...just her. What we later found out was that the woman hated kids and was doing it for the extra money. So that food was the cheapest meal you could dish up...a tin of pilchards and dry bread.

B

If you were a child with glasses or with spots, you were always left till the end.

We were told to sit quietly on the floor while the villagers and farmers' wives came to choose which children they wanted. I noticed boys of about 12 went very quickly – perhaps to help on the farm? Eventually only my friend Nancy and myself were left – two plain, straight-haired little girls wearing glasses, now rather tearful.

A large, happy-looking, middle-aged lady rushed in asking, 'Is that all you have left?' A sad, slow nod of the head from the teacher. 'I'll take the poor bairns.' We were led out of the hall with this stranger and taken to a farm where we spent two years.

C

We didn't know anything about nature and we ran after the peacocks and tore the tail feathers from them to send home to our mum. We were 48 children and they only had billets for 46. The rich man of the village said he didn't want any evacuees and his son lived next door. When the vicar explained they had two boys he agreed to take one and the son took the other boy.

So I spent two and a half years living in his big house. We were driven there by the vicar the next day and I'd never been in a car before. On the gear-lever was a diagram that I thought was a swastika. So when we got to the house we told him that the man who drove us had a swastika in his car. So the local bobby went round to interrogate the vicar.

D

The journey seemed to take for ever. It can't have done though, because as I found out later we were only 85 miles from home. It's funny but I can remember that journey so well. We got tired of counting fields as we passed them – for many it was the first time they had seen fields. I was just a little more fortunate. I was once taken out into the country. I can remember though how we had to cross a viaduct, how frightened we all were in case the train should come off the rails and we would all fall into the water underneath. You should have heard the sighs of relief when we crossed safely.

Reading Games, © Jill Hadfield and Charles Hadfield 1995

E

The couple were quite old – maybe around 50, which seemed old then. She had greasy hair in a plait and used to ask me to braid it for her. I hated doing it. If we were sick we had to wait until money arrived from our parents before she would get medicine. We weren't allowed in the house till 5pm and in the evenings had to sit in the scullery with its stone floor. She said the alternative to us was a couple of Irish labourers, otherwise she would never have consented to our living there. I think she was trying to save money on the allowance given her. We became very thin. From 7 to 9 at night we met with two other girls, similarly treated, and would sit in the bushes, around a fire if we could steal matches, talking about when we got home...

F

Smut the cat, Joey the canary and a large tortoise we had had for 16 years...what were we to do with them? There was only one thing left and that was to have them put to sleep.

I bravely put Smut into a box, the tortoise in a bag on my back and the cage in the other hand. I walked along the Hastings seafront to a vet's. I can tell you how much I hated Hitler.

Putting my sad cargo down to have a rest and have a cry, I was aware of a soldier staring. He asked what was wrong and when I told him he offered to help.

Only the tortoise never did get to the vet's – instead we put him in the local park flowerbeds. But sadly we joined a long queue at the vet's. People were all forced to do the same. Sorrowfully we walked back empty-handed.

G

I was terribly unhappy there and I remember a day when it was raining hard and she sent me outside. She bolted the door and I crawled into the chicken-house full of straw, and I stayed there until she came out and brought me in. She didn't want me in the place you see.

This other little girl's daddy was a soldier and one day the lady said to me, 'You're to go upstairs and stay in the room and don't come down.' And she got Margaret Rose ready and made her pretty and she locked my door.

I could hear them talking in the kitchen below and I got a pencil and a piece of paper, wrote a little note: 'Please tell my mummy to come and get me' and I dropped it out of the window.

About a week after that I was on my way to school. There was a thick fog and I could hear footsteps coming towards me on the other side of the road. And I suddenly heard my mum saying, 'Is that you Mary?' and I said, 'Oh, Mum,' and I went dashing across the road and she was quite horrified when she saw me. She took me back to the house and told the woman exactly what she thought of her and she said, 'How dare you send my daughter out on a morning like this. She's got holes in her shoes and no coat on. I'll make sure you never get any more kids to look after, after the way you treated her.'

H

My sister and I devised a plan. We knew that Mrs Hudson read our letters from home before she gave them to us to read, and she insisted on reading the letters we sent to our parents before she would give us a stamp to post them. We therefore wrote to our parents telling them how unhappy we were and left the unsealed letter in our bedroom. We didn't have to wait long before our plan showed results. The same day we returned from afternoon school to find our belongings in the front garden and we had no reply to our banging on the front door.

We went to tell our story to the headmaster, who lived a short distance away. He returned with us and knocked on Mrs Hudson's front door but found no response. He picked up our bags and took us to the sea-front where he deposited my sister and me with the bags and told us he would try and get accommodation for the night.

We must have looked an unhappy pair. A lady came along with a dog and she asked us what was wrong. We told her our tale and she sat beside us and promised that we could go home with her and stay with her as long as we wanted. When the headmaster returned he was overjoyed as he had found it impossible to find any accommodation for us.

Reading Games, © Jill Hadfield and Charles Hadfield 1995

Fill in the blanks in these extracts from the children's letters home.

......and all we had for supper was .... and when we asked
.... we got a
....

.... boys of 12 were chosen very quickly, but we were left till the end
because ....

.... the rich man in the vilage said he didn't want any children, but
the vicar told him about us, so now I live with................................. and my
brother lives with...

.... the train crossed a viaduct and we were all frightened
in case..

.... I don't like the woman. She has greasy hair in a ....
....and she asks me to ....We're not
allowed in the house until .... and if we're sick we have to wait
until .... before ....

.... I was so sad when I had to take Smut, Joey, and the tortoise
to ...., but I met a .... who helped me. We
didn't take ....to the............................... . Instead we
....

I'm very unhappy here. One day it was raining and she sent me
.... I crawled into .... and stayed there
until .... I've got......................... in my shoes and no
....

I was very unhappy with Mrs Hudson because she always read
.... So one day we
.... and when we came home from school we found
.... But the headmaster took us to the
.... where we met a .... who promised
....

Reading Games, © Jill Hadfield and Charles Hadfield 1995

A Take a break

A friend of a friend, out on a shopping expedition, was in need of refreshment.

So, laden down with her purchases, she found a cafeteria and bought herself a refreshing cup of tea and a Kit-Kat. The place was so full the only seat she could find was opposite a scruffy punk reading the paper, but she put her bags down and relaxed.

Apparently, as she did so, the punk folded up his paper, reached forward for the Kit-Kat, broke off half and shoved it in his mouth.

The woman was taken aback and quite speechless, but the punk ignored her, and a minute later he picked up the rest of the bar and finished it.

By now the woman was furious. Fuming, she reached forward for the punk's cream cake, took a massive bite, then threw it back down on the table, before gathering up her bags and storming out of the cafeteria.

Still angry, she decided to catch the first bus home, felt in her pocket for her travelcard, and found her own Kit-Kat intact.

B A nasty set-to

One of my uncle's mates got a job for a building company driving a huge cement mixer truck.

Driving the monster truck thrilled him to bits, but working on big ready-mix jobs often kept him away from home for days at a time. And although he loved his young wife dearly, he became convinced she was having an affair. It was the little things: she'd started wearing new clothes and too much perfume.

Apparently, in an effort to catch her out, he drove home early one day. Sure enough, there was a brand new red soft-top sports car parked outside the house, and the upstairs curtains were closed.

Wiping a tear from his eye with his fist, he backed up his truck, and filled the car to the brim with quick-setting cement.

Job done, he hid round the corner to see what would happen. Sure enough, his wife came out of the house with a man in a suit. They looked together at the ruined car and his wife burst into tears. The husband was surprised to see the man shrug his shoulders, bid his wife goodbye and climb into a completely different car.

Jumping out of his truck he marched to confront his wife and found out the truth. The car was a surprise present she had bought him: the man was the salesman who'd just delivered it!

Reading Games, © Jill Hadfield and Charles Hadfield 1995

C A low note

One of our old dinner ladies from school was chattering on the corner of a busy road when she saw a driver, veering from side to side, collide with a stationary motor.

Expecting the driver to carry on regardless, as so many people seem to do in this day and age, she and others in the street were pleasantly surprised to see the considerate driver stop, earnestly examine the damage and take a pen and paper from his car and write down the details. He then placed the note under the damaged car's windscreen wiper before driving on.

A minute later, the owner of the damaged car appeared. He was distressed to see his dented wing but pleased to see the note, which he read carefully.

Then he exploded. The passer-by said she'd witnessed the accident and asked what the matter was: didn't he have the other driver's details on the note?

D Phone home

A double-glazing salesman in south London was ringing a contact telephone number he'd been given, and the receiver was picked up immediately at the other end. A tiny voice whispered:

'Hallo?'

'Hallo, can I speak to your daddy please?' said the caller.

'No, he's busy,' replied the little voice.

'Your mummy, then. I'll speak to her.'

'You can't. She's busy too.'

'Is there anyone else there?' persisted the caller.

'Yes,' the voice conceded, 'a policeman, but he's busy as well.'

'Anyone else?' The caller was now getting a little exasperated.

'Yes, a social worker.'

'Well, can I speak to the social worker, then?'

'No, she's busy too,' said the soft little voice.

'Look, you've got all those people at your house and they're all busy. What are they *doing*?' asked the caller.

'See for yourself,' muttered the angry owner, showing her the paper, which read:

'I've just crunched your car, and because there are loads of nosy people watching me, I'm pretending to write down my name, registration number and insurance details.'

'Looking for me,' came the whispered reply.

E Signed, sealed and delivered

The father of a boy I went to school with was a police sergeant – and was once called out to the scene of an armed robbery, a high street bank.

The cashier told him a nasty-looking bloke in a trench-coat had entered the bank, come over to his window and pushed a dog-eared envelope under the glass.

The bank clerk squinted at the childish scrawl on the back of the envelope. The note read, 'GIV US ALL THE MUNNY, IVE GOT A GUN'.

He looked up to find himself staring down the barrel of a pistol. The cashier complied immediately, thrusting the money over the counter, which the robber shoved into his greedy holdall.

The thief himself had only just arrived home and started excitedly to count his booty, when the police burst through the door.

The robber threw his arms in the air immediately, but was baffled by the efficiency of the police on the case. 'How did you track me down so fast?' he wailed.

'Quite simple, Mastermind,' the sergeant sneered, snapping on the bracelets. 'Your name and address were on the other side of the envelope.'

F An unfair cop

A friend's father is a sergeant in the Police Constabulary.

This was well before the days of joyriders and serial killers: criminals in those days were an altogether nicer breed and one of his colleagues told him about an interesting experience. The policeman was patrolling a particularly ill-lit street. With his torch blazing, he flashed into each doorway looking for trouble.

It was just as well, because his vigilance soon paid off. The flashlight illuminated the front of a cosy old tobacconist's with the door slightly ajar.

Steeling himself for possible violent confrontation, he slowly pushed open the door. Nothing appeared to be wrong, so, radioing the station, the policeman poked around the shop. Then he checked no one was looking and helped himself to 200 cigarettes, which he hid under his helmet.

The flustered shopowner arrived shortly, bursting with gratitude, and after checking his goods he praised the policeman's diligence and dedication to the job. Then he insisted on giving the officer a little 'thank you' for his trouble. 'Here, take these two hundred ciggies,' he offered.

'No, no, sir that really won't be necessary, I'm only doing my job,' the bobby protested uncomfortably. 'Anyway, I don't have anywhere to put them.'

'Nonsense,' replied the shopkeeper, reaching up. 'You can hide them under your helmet.'

Reading Games, © Jill Hadfield and Charles Hadfield 1995

G Tow job

One of the first places to have the automatic video speedchecks fitted was at Wembley on London's north circular road.

Recently a motorist known to a friend was quite taken aback to receive a summons from the police advising him that following the examination of photographic evidence, he was being fined for exceeding the speed limit.

The thing was, his car had broken down on the morning of the date stated, so he demanded to see the pictures for himself.

Down at the station, he was shown the prints, which indeed showed his car crossing a junction at considerable speed and with the light on red.

But, as the driver pointed out, the photo missed out a crucial point.

H Fitted up wardrobe

A man who lives round the corner left his keys with a neighbour while he and his family went on holiday to Frinton.

The neighbour, a conscientious chap, took his responsibility very seriously, keeping an eye on the property at all times.

When a furniture van turned up on the Wednesday to deliver a new wardrobe, the neighbour let them in, signed for the furniture, and kept an eye on the deliverymen while they were inside the property.

They seemed pleasant enough chaps – he wasn't really surprised when they turned up again the next day saying they'd delivered the wrong piece and would have to take it back. He left them to it, watched them leave, and again locked up carefully.

But when the family returned from down south, they found everything they had – video, TV, jewellery, microwave – was missing.

The police arrived and questioned the neighbour intensely. He racked his brains but could not recall nothing out of the ordinary apart from the slight problem with the wardrobe.

The officers nodded knowingly. 'That's happening all over town,' they explained.

He was being towed by a breakdown truck at the time.

Apparently, a diminutive villain hides in the wardrobe when it's delivered. Then he fills it up with consumer collectables overnight, and his accomplices remove him and the booty along with the 'wrong' wardrobe the next day.

Reading Games, © Jill Hadfield and Charles Hadfield 1995

Dorothy Parker

US writer, critic, wit

1   And on hearing that President Coolidge, a man of few words and even less action, was dead, she inquired, '*****'.

2   Then asked what she thought of a certain woman, she breathed, feigning admiration, '*****'.

Sir Noël Coward

Terribly, terribly witty actor/playwright

3   A dim-witted impresario, no friend of Coward's, blew his brains out. When told, the playwright remarked, '*****'.

4   Asked his opinion of a play featuring a child 'prodigy', Coward remarked, '*****'.

Oscar Wilde

Aesthete, writer, wit

5   Wilde, like Churchill, could make a would-be insulter look quite foolish. Receiving bouquets in a theatre foyer one night, he suddenly found himself presented with a rotten cabbage. He took it, smiled and said, '*****'.

6   A customs officer once asked him if he had anything to declare. '*****'.

7   Asked his opinion of a truly awful play, he replied, '*****'.

James Whistler

US painter, friendly foe of Wilde

8   Whistler often got his own back on Wilde. On the one occasion, after a particularly scintillating remark from the artist, Wilde exclaimed, 'I wish I had said that!'
'*****' said Whistler.

9   A well-known bore tried to engage him in conversation: 'You know, Mr Whistler, I passed your house last night–'
'*****' said Whistler.

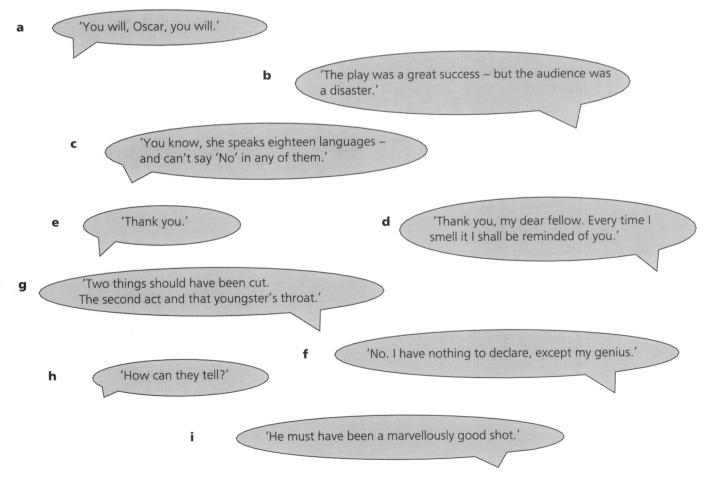

a   'You will, Oscar, you will.'

b   'The play was a great success – but the audience was a disaster.'

c   'You know, she speaks eighteen languages – and can't say 'No' in any of them.'

e   'Thank you.'

d   'Thank you, my dear fellow. Every time I smell it I shall be reminded of you.'

g   'Two things should have been cut. The second act and that youngster's throat.'

f   'No. I have nothing to declare, except my genius.'

h   'How can they tell?'

i   'He must have been a marvellously good shot.'

Reading Games, © Jill Hadfield and Charles Hadfield 1995

A Being mistaken for his own gardener one day, a nosey woman asked **Groucho Marx** how much he was paid. 'Oh, I don't get paid in dollars,' he replied simply. 'The lady of the house just lets me sleep with her.'

B Warner Brothers threatened legal action over the proposed title of his next picture, 'A Night in Casablanca', arguing that it was too close to their own 'Casablanca'. **Groucho Marx** told them. 'I'll sue you for using the word "Brothers."'

C And asked what he thought of the latest Victor Mature/Hedy Lamarr film, **Groucho Marx** answered, 'You can't expect the public to get excited about a film where the leading man's bust is bigger than the leading lady's.'

D A drunk lurched up to **Groucho Marx**, patted him on the back and said, 'You old son-of-a-gun, – you probably don't remember me.' Groucho snapped, 'I never forget a face but in your case I'll be glad to make an exception.'

E **Churchill** was one of the few people to get the better of Shaw. The latter invited him to the first night of his play, enclosing two tickets. 'One for yourself and one for a friend – if you have one.' Churchill wrote back, saying he couldn't make it, but could he have tickets for the second night – 'If there is one.'

F And when a very old man, on one of his increasingly rare visits to the House of Commons, an MP remarked of him, 'After all, they say he's potty.' 'They say he can't hear either,' muttered **Churchill**.

G The young man who photographed him on his 80th birthday said courteously that he hoped to do the same on his hundredth. 'I don't see why not,' said **Churchill**. 'You look reasonably fit to me.'

H And to a female MP who once rebuked him for being intoxicated at a dinner party, **Churchill** retorted, 'And you, madam, are ugly. But I shall be sober tomorrow.'

I On the subject of an ill-received play, the newly successful **Shaw** was cabled by a producer now offering to stage the same work he'd earlier rejected. Shaw cabled back: 'Better never than late.'
.

J And while at a party, **Shaw** was noticed standing alone in a corner. His hostess anxiously enquired if he was enjoying himself. 'Certainly,' he replied. 'There is nothing else here to enjoy.'

K **Shaw**, once a music critic, was in a restaurant which boasted a tone-deaf orchestra. Its leader recognised him and sent a note asking what he would like them to play next. 'Dominoes,' replied Shaw.

L Another would-be hostess sent **Shaw** the pompous invitation: 'Lady Blank will be at home on Tuesday between four and six o'clock.' Back it came, bearing Shaw's scribbled reply: 'Mr Bernard Shaw likewise.'

M **Picasso**, like Whistler, despaired of poor design, in his case his own. A visitor once found him staring disconsolately at a painting on the easel so, to cheer him up, said 'It's a masterpiece.' 'No, the nose is all wrong,' Picasso said. 'It throws the whole picture out of perspective.' 'Then why not alter the nose?' 'Impossible,' sighed Picasso. 'I can't find it.'

N An American GI told **Picasso** he didn't like modern paintings because they weren't realistic, then went on to show him a snapshot of his girlfriend. 'My, is she really as small as that?' asked Picasso.

O Asked why he had none of his own paintings on the walls of his house, **Picasso** replied, 'I can't afford them.'

P **Picasso** went to see his local cabinetmaker for a new wardrobe and drew a quick sketch of what he wanted on a sheet of paper. He gave the sketch to the cabinetmaker and asked how much it would cost. 'Nothing at all,' replied the craftsman. 'Just sign the sketch.'

1 'How much are you paid?'

' ....
.... '

2 'Your title, *A Night in Casablanca*, is too close to our title, *Casablanca*.'

' ....
....
.... '

3 'What do you think of the latest Victor Mature/Hedy Lamarr film?'

' ....
.... '

4 'You old son-of-a-gun, you probably don't remember me.'

' ....
.... '

5 'One for yourself and one for a friend if you have one.'

' ....
.... '

6 'After all, they say he's potty.'

' ....
.... '

7 'I hope to photograph you again on your hundredth birthday.'

' ....
.... '

8 'You're drunk.'

' ....
.... '

9 'I will stage your play.'

' ....
.... '

10 'Are you enjoying yourself?'

' ....
.... '

11 'What would you like us to play next?'

' ....
.... '

12 'Lady Blank will be at home on Tuesday between four and six o'clock.'

' ....
.... '

13 'It's a masterpiece'

' .... '

'Then why not alter the nose?'

' .... '

14 'I don't like modern paintings because they aren't realistic.'

' ....
.... '

15 'Why don't you have any of your own paintings on your walls?'

' ....
.... '

16 'How much will it cost?'

' ....
.... '

BODY LANGUAGE

A light-hearted look at some of the deadly, but unintentional, gaffes that can so easily occur when cultures collide at Heathrow, the world's premier international airport.

I'm never bored at airports. Quite the reverse. I visit them like other people go to the ballet. To a Manwatcher, there's nothing more fascinating than observing citizens of different countries mingling and exchanging body signals.

And nowhere is the performance so enjoyable as at Heathrow, the world's top international airport.

Day and night they pour in, a cast of 36 million a year from every corner of the globe.

Where else but Heathrow could you hope to see Brazilians rubbing shoulders with Brahmins, Poles with Polynesians, Madagascans with Minnesotans and Neapolitans with Nepalese?

Intelligence or stupidity? It depends whether you're Dutch.

Each nationality has its own language of posture and gesture. But since these body-lingos are often mutually incomprehensible, an innocent gesture made in an airport lounge may well be an unwitting insult.

To find out more about the eye-pull, the ear-tug, and the celebrated Greek 'moutza', now read on …

A

Happily, I can report the BAA's information staff are trained in body language.

A Sardinian woman asks if it is easy to find a taxi at Heathrow. The answer she gets is a cheery British thumbs up. (Very likely from one of the 900 cabbies who serve the airport on an average day.) Immediately, she clonks the unfortunate man with her handbag for making such a devastatingly insulting suggestion. This is why, incidentally, it's not a very good idea to thumb a lift in Sardinia.

Isn't there at least one truly international gesture? Don't bet on it.

A Japanese asks an American passenger whether Heathrow has a luggage trolley service. It has. And as it happens, this service is not only first class, but FREE! So the Yank replies with the famous 'A-OK' ring gesture. But to the Japanese this signifies 'money' and he concludes there is a large charge for the service. Meanwhile, a Tunisian on-looker thinks the American is telling the Japanese that he is a worthless rogue and he is going to kill him.

In Japan it means 'money'.

In America this means 'A-OK'.

In Tunisia it means 'I'll kill you'.

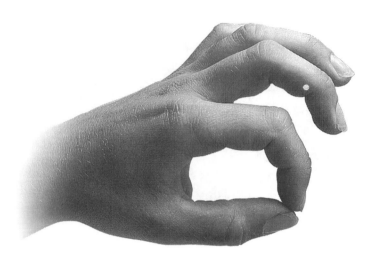

B

It is so easy to give offence. Suppose a passenger asks at the Information Desk where he should go to pay his airport tax.

Now the good news is that at Heathrow, unlike many airports I could name, passengers don't pay any taxes. But just as the Information Assistant begins to say so, she is assailed by a tremendous itch and tugs at her earlobe.

Astonishing though it may seem, this simple gesture means five different things in five different Mediterranean countries.

Depending on his nationality, the Assistant has offered the passenger the following insult:

TO A SPANIARD: 'You rotten sponger'.

TO A GREEK: 'You'd better watch it, mate'.

TO A MALTESE: 'You're a sneaky little so-and-so'.

TO AN ITALIAN: 'Get lost you pansy.'

Only a Portuguese (to whom the gesture signifies something ineffably wonderful) would hang around long enough to hear the answer.

This means five different things (four of them insulting) in five different countries.

Reading Games, © Jill Hadfield and Charles Hadfield 1995

C

In France it means 'zero'.

The ring-gesture can have further meanings.

A Frenchman has just read a BAA advertisement. Glancing around the restaurant in Terminal 4, he remarks wonderingly to his wife, 'You know how much zis aeroport cost the British taxpayer? Not a sou'. And he makes the finger and thumb ring which to him means 'zero'.

Unfortunately, at the time he is glancing at a Colombian who is enjoying a fine Burgundy with his steak Bearnaise. The Colombian, enraged by the deadly obscenity which he assumes is directed at him, chokes on his wine and catches at his nose with finger and thumb.

This appalls a Syrian sitting opposite, who thinks the Colombian is telling him to 'go to hell'.

The Syrian is restrained with difficulty by his Greek colleague from getting up and punching the Colombian on the nose. Meanwhile the *maître d'* hurries over and attempts to calm the situation with two out-thrust palms. This of course is taken by the Greek to be a double-'moutza' and in his rage he promptly skewers the unfortunate man with his fish knife.

D

Something in your eye? Think before you touch the lower lid. If a Saudi sees you, he'll think you're calling him stupid, but a South American señorita will think you're making a pass at her.

There is no greater insult you can offer a Greek than to thrust your palms towards his face. This gesture, called the 'moutza', is descended from the old Byzantine custom of smearing filth from the gutter in the faces of condemned criminals as they were led in chains through the city.

So vile is this insult that in Greece even the Churchillian Victory-V is taboo, as it looks like a half-'moutza'.

Thus the Cretan or Athenian traveller, ordering two teas in a Heathrow restaurant, will carefully reverse his palm and give the waiter two fingers.

With 22,600 orders for cups of tea open to misinterpretation every day, the wonder is the place functions at all.

**To a Saudi this is insulting.
To a South American it is meant to be flattering.**

Reading Games, © Jill Hadfield and Charles Hadfield 1995

Answer as many questions as you can and then ask other students for help.

1 What is a 'moutza'?

2 What is a 'Victory V'?

3 Where would 'two fingers' be an insult?

4 Why is it inadvisable to thumb a lift in Sardinia?

5 What does a 'thumbs-up' sign mean in Britain?

6 What would a Syrian think if you held your nose?

7 a Where would this be insulting?
   b Where in the world might a man make this gesture to a woman?

8 What does this mean:
   a in France?
   b in America?
   c in Japan?
   d in Tunisia?
   e in Columbia?

9 Translate the above gesture into
   a Spanish
   b Greek
   c Maltese
   d Italian
   e Portuguese

1 A cross–section of British children and their grandparents were interviewed on the topics listed below. Their answers showed how much attitudes have changed in the last 50 years. Before you read their answers discuss with a partner how **you** think children's lives and attitudes have changed over the last 50 years.

Now put a–k to match the texts with the topics.

	50 years ago	Today
Kids and Clothes		
Kids and Games		
Kids and Money		
Kids and Transport		
Kids and Home		
Kids and Holidays		
Kids and Discipline		
Kids and Bedtime		
Kids and Food		
Kids and Music		
Kids and School		

2 Choose the headings which apply to your text. Write them down on the back of this paper and make brief notes under each heading.

buying clothes

father's role in family life

boys' clothes

difference in status of boys and girls

mother's role in family life

shoes

sleeping arrangements

baby minding

girls' jobs and duties

punishments – girls – boys

girls' hairstyles

children and adult conversation

boys' hairstyles

boys' jobs and duties

behaviour at meals

family size

Then ask the others in your group for information about the other headings.

50 years ago

50 years ago: Families were larger, working hours longer and incomes lower. Most fathers were in full time employment, but there was little work for women, and those who helped by taking in washing or sewing felt a sense of shame. Most people lived in rented or council property, without bathrooms, indoor toilets, electricity or hot water. But you could leave your home unlocked – vandalism was non-existent and policemen were respected. Children were safe on the streets, too – sexual attacks were unheard of.

A

50 years ago: Foreign holidays were unknown. Working men had only two weeks' holiday a year and often it was unpaid. Most families took working holidays and that included the children.

B

50 years ago: A big issue. Parents, teachers, policemen and relatives all worked together to instil respect or fear in children. At home, the father's word was law and if children were caught doing something wrong, they were beaten with belts.

C

50 years ago: There were a lot of make-believe games and children entertained themselves by making up games. They played with friends, brothers and sisters and one of their favourites was dressing-up. Funfairs were special – they'd walk around and decide which ride they'd go on.

D

50 years ago: It was porridge for breakfast and bread and jam for tea after school. Best meal was the Sunday roast. Salads, fruit and poultry were rare and favourite treats were cakes and home-made ginger beer.

E

50 years ago: Children had three sets of clothes – best for church, second best for school and old clothes for playing – all in dull colours and often itchy material. Most were home-made and mended for as long as possible before being handed down to younger siblings. 'My father always sent me to school in shoes,' said one 60-year-old – boots were a social stigma.

F

50 years ago: Very few children received pocket money regularly. They earned pennies by returning empty bottles and jam jars and running errands, but were rarely paid for helping in the house. Children spent their earned money immediately in case it was taken from them by their parents. Many rushed straight to the sweet shop (a Milky Bar was a treat, as it was very rich) and they'd suck their chocolate bars to make them last longer. They also spent their money on comics and trips to the cinema.

G

50 years ago: Bicycles were used by adults and teenagers, but were too expensive to give to 10-year-olds. They walked to and from school, and came home for lunch – children would often walk several miles a day. Private cars were rare, and many couldn't afford to use public transport regularly.

H

50 years ago: The three Rs were all important and children had regular spelling and mental arithmetic tests. The 11-plus was their big academic hurdle and they left school at 14 or 15.

I

50 years ago: There was no music aimed specifically at children. They listened to their parents' choice on the wireless or wind-up gramophone. They liked listening to Gracie Fields, George Formby and Shirley Temple.

J

50 years ago: Children got up at 6.30–7.30 a.m., ate breakfast and walked to school. After school, they played with their brothers and sisters and helped in the home. With no television, a cold house and poor light, bedtime was early – 7 to 7.30 p.m. Monday was washing day and children helped to wring clothes. On Tuesday, the house was 'full of steam' as the washing dried. Cleaning day was Friday and one day was set aside for baking.

K

Reading Games, © Jill Hadfield and Charles Hadfield 1995

Today

A   **Today:** They get up as late as 8.30 a.m., and go to bed between 8.30 and 10.30 p.m. The days are differentiated according to television programmes and after-school activities. Any children who have to look after younger brothers and sisters describe them as 'pests' or a 'menace'.

B   **Today:** Children have new bicycles which they've bought or received as presents. But because of the dangers on the roads, they're only used for play in quiet streets and not as a means of transport. Almost every family has a car, and parents mostly drive their children to school.

C   **Today:** Children are rich by comparison, with between 50p and £3.50 a week to spend as they like. Pocket money is supplemented by money earned from washing up, tidying their bedrooms or helping with the gardening. Most children have bank and building society accounts, and they save for large items like stereos, TVs and clothes.

D   **Today:** Homes are comparatively well equipped and comfortable. The luxury of a bathroom and toilet are taken for granted. Fathers in work are more likely to be in a service industry or self-employed. Mothers work full or part-time, but many feel guilty. Children can't go out whenever and wherever they like because of the amount of traffic and the fear of attack.

E   **Today:** Children have their own stereo systems or Walkmans. They hear music on the television, videos, records, tapes and radios. Five Star and Madonna are the current favourites.

F   **Today:** Many children find school 'boring'. Their favourite lessons are maths and computer studies.

G   **Today:** Children look forward to their annual family holidays. Self-catering, camping and villa holidays are popular. They usually go somewhere different every year, travelling by plane or car, and the majority of 10-year-olds have been abroad at least once.

H   **Today:** Kids wear a large variety of casual clothes in bright colours. No one talks about wearing hand-me-downs. There are special 'best' clothes, and new outfits are bought throughout the year. T-shirts, jeans, track suits and training shoes are all popular among 10-year-olds.

I   **Today:** Children expect to be entertained and often complain of being bored. Most prefer to play on their own in their rooms with a computerised game. Nearly all love going to funfairs, but aren't happy unless they have a ride on everything.

J   **Today:** A non-issue. Most children expect to be able to 'get away with anything'. If they're cheeky or misbehave, they're generally sent to their rooms, but it isn't a deterrent. It's no longer a case of children being seen and not heard: adults speak more to children these days and discuss many things openly in front of them.

K   **Today:** If children eat breakfast at all, they munch cereal and then have lunch at school. There are no fixed meal times and fewer family meals. They often help themselves to snacks if hungry and eat in front of the TV. Families eat out often and convenience foods and take-aways are popular.

SIX IN THE BED

Large families were common, and homes were small and crowded. This usually meant sharing not only a room but also a bed with a number of brothers and sisters. A London man, Mr Forbes, remembers his childhood in Islington in the early 1900s:

'We had all the boys in one bed – six of us lined up with three at the top and three at the bottom. My four sisters shared the other bed and that filled the room. There was a curtain across the middle and when my eldest sister got bigger she slept in the living room or at my aunt's nearby.'

It was quite common for older children to go and live with relatives for a while when space became a problem at home. Children were often sent out of the house to play because there just wasn't room for everyone to be in the home at once.

Most children probably saw much more of their mothers than their fathers. Working hours were very long and by the time a man got home he was very tired or the children were in bed:

'My father, he didn't have a lot to do with us really. I mean he was at work all day. He was strict, strict to a certain extent but it was mother really who brought us up. My father was at work and when he used to come home it was bedtime nearly for us you see, and we didn't see a right lot of him.'

Elizabeth Roberts, 'Working-Class Women in the North West'

Since working men had little time or opportunity to be involved with bringing up the family it was considered a woman's, not a man's job. But in industrial towns many women went out to full-time work too. There were no nurseries or crêches, and babyminding was usually done by a relative or neighbour – often a very young girl or an elderly woman. Because the working day was ten hours or more it was difficult for mothers to organise babyminding:

'I myself had some very hard times, as I had to go out to work in the mill and put the baby out to nurse. I had to get up by four in the morning, and get my baby out of bed, wash and dress it, and then leave home by five, as I had half an hour's walk to take my baby to my mother's, and then go to my work and stand all day till half past five at night and then walk home again with my baby. I had to do this with three of them.'

Margaret Llewelyn Davies (ed) *Maternity*

Many politicians and doctors blamed working mothers for neglecting their children, believing that men should work and women should stay at home. This statement is a typical one for the times. 'For a mother to work outside the home is in every respect an individual mistake, a social tragedy, a communal blunder.' Child Welfare Conference, 1890s.

In fact many families could not survive without the mother's as well as the father's income. And this is still true of many families today.

LIFE WAS HARD

Life was hard and rough for working people in Britain at the end of the last century. From a very early age children were expected to do all they could to help their parents, in order that the family could survive, as this description of a country childhood in the 1870s illustrates:

> **'Boys fed poultry and pigs and soon were milking and cutting firewood. By eight years they could do much more than all that. Girls had to bath little brother and sister just a size smaller than themselves and stagger with pails of water from the tap fifty yards away when scarcely taller than the pails they carried between them. To 'help' was the price of contact with beloved and admired parents; even tiny ones understood that our parents could not 'manage' without us.'**

> **Mabel Ashby, *Joseph Ashby of Tysoe***

In working-class families girls were responsible for looking after the younger children while their mothers were busy. One writer described the girls in the East End of London in the 1880s as 'little mothers':

> **'At the open door sits a girl of eight ... a typical 'little mother' of the London doorstep ... She is nursing a heavy baby who is perhaps a year old. She talks to it, soothes it, hushes it to sleep, rocks it, dandles it when it wakes up, and kisses its poor little face again and again. But every other minute her attention is distracted by the conduct of a sister, aged four, and a brother, aged five, who are also under her guardianship ... Because she is the oldest of all that have come, all that come after are hers to tend and hers to watch. By the time she marries and has children of her own she will be a woman weary of motherhood.'**

> **George Sims, *How the Poor Live***

This writer, brought up at the turn of the century, describes his duties as a young boy:

> **'I could milk a cow by the time I was seven years old and when eight I earned sixpence a day at harvest time for 'stanarding' – that is holding the horse still by its head while sheaves of corn were loaded on the cart. I would walk on at a command, then on the word 'stanard' I would stop. It meant 'stand hard' or still. Then at the end of the week I would line up with the men to get my pay. Most I gave to Mum to help buy boots which wore away quickly on the gritty country roads.'**

> **George Noakes, *To be a Farmer's Boy***

CHILDREN SHOULD BE SEEN AND NOT HEARD

Old people's memories:

'I once answered my mother back and she boxed my ears for it. I never did it again.'

'You weren't allowed to chatter. If spoken to you spoke back, but having too much to say wasn't allowed.'

In both rich and poor families, parents seem to have been strict about children's behaviour, for example, silence at meals was a common rule: only 'please' and 'thank you' were allowed. Fussiness over food was not tolerated – you had to eat everything you were given or it was served up for the next meal. There was no choice either and little variety; many children got bread and margarine or jam for most of their meals. Children were often taught to say grace – or at least in front of visitors. Maud Pember Reeves described her visit to the home of Mrs P, in London at the beginning of this century:

'When in the visitor's presence the little P's have swallowed a hasty dinner, which may consist of a plateful of 'stoo' or perhaps a suet pudding and treacle, taken standing, they never omit to close their eyes and say 'Thang Gord fer me good dinner – good afternoon Mrs R,' before they go. Mrs P would call them back if they did not say that.'

Maud Pember Reeves, *Round About a Pound a Week*

Adult discussions were considered unsuitable for children. Many people remember being forbidden to read the newspapers or having to leave the room when adults were talking. Children were expected to know their place in the world – after adults – and in this order of things boys came before girls. Parents may have been stricter with their daughters than with their sons, as Molly Hughes describes:

'My father's slogan was that boys should go everywhere and know everything and that a girl should stay at home and know nothing. The boys used to go to the theatre and music halls. Mother explained that they were not dull, only not very nice. It made no difference to me what they were like since I was never allowed to go even to a theatre.'

Molly Hughes, *A London Child of the 1870s*

When it came to punishments it seems that boys were more likely to be beaten than girls. This writer vividly remembers his mother's policy:

'A common feature of the time was a length of leather hanging on the kitchen cupboard for the chastisement of children. "For bad boys," my mother told us, "a yard of strap is worth a mile of talk."'

Robert Roberts, *A Ragged Schooling*

A minor crime could lead to harsh punishment. Grace Foakes described what happened when her brother stole a twopenny lamp:

'He took Robert into the bedroom, locking the door after him. He made him strip and gave him a terrible beating with the belt he wore round his waist. I shall never forget Robert's cries or my mother's tears. He was black and blue with bruises next morning ... I do not think Robert ever forgave my father.'

Grace Foakes, Between High Walls

D

APPEARANCES

In most working-class families money was too scarce to buy new clothes, and only the eldest got bargains from the second-hand stall, or things made by their mothers. The younger ones wore 'hand-me-downs' which were often too big, patched and mended, and much hated. Being in fashion was simply out of the question. Photographs taken at the time show how common it was for children to play in the street and to go to school barefoot because their parents couldn't afford to buy shoes.

Before they started school, boys and girls had to share and swap clothes and in fact all boys including those in well-off families, wore dresses until they were 'breeched' – i.e. given their first pair of trousers at about the age of three.

'We were all in skirts in those days. We only started to wear knickers (trousers) when we started school, so we all looked very much alike.'

George Noakes, *To be a Farmer's Boy*

Hairstyles were a different matter. Girls usually had long hair while boys wore theirs cropped short. Grace Foakes, who grew up in the East End of London at the turn of the century, describes hers:

'Every Friday night at bath time my mother would wash our heads with soda, water and Sunlight soap, and then plait it into many plaits. These would not be undone until Sunday, when they were loosed, crimped and shining. My brothers went to a barber who would give them what was a called a 'prison crop'. Every bit of hair was shaved off. This was very cold in winter but the hair took longer to grow if cut this way.'

Grace Foakes, *Between High Walls*

A   New Year's Day: *1 January*

The year should begin happily, they say, so that it will end happily, and on the first morning of the new year children in Scotland, Wales, and the English border counties rise early so that they may make the round of their friends and neighbours. 'On January 1st,' writes a 13-year-old Scottish girl, 'I always go New Year's Gifting with my sister and friends, about four of us. I get up about 7 o'clock and call for my friends and go round the houses and farms.' They sing (although Christmas is seven days old):

I wish you a merry Christmas,
A happy New Year,
A pocket full of money
And a cellar full of beer,
A good fat pig
To last you all the year –
Please to give me a New Year's Gift
For this New Year.

'We do not always get money, we sometimes have mincepies or apples.' Nevertheless they collect 'nine or ten shillings every year', although gifting must be finished by midday. 'You must be gone before twelve o'clock or they will call you a fool and the people won't give you anything, and when the people see you next time they will all shout fool at you.' In some villages, such as Bleddfa and Llangunllo, the girls save their gifting money and keep it for a special outing.

Across the border in England, children also call at houses, visiting as many of the scattered homesteads as they can, reciting:

Happy New Year! Happy New Year!
I've come to wish you a Happy New Year.
I've got a little pocket and it is very thin,
Please give me a penny to put some money in.
If you haven't got a penny, a halfpenny will do,
If you haven't got a halfpenny, well –
God Bless You!

B   Shrove Tuesday
(the day before 'Ash Wednesday')

For centuries Shrove Tuesday has been a day of high festival for apprentices and schoolchildren. It has been a day of feasting, cock fighting, and throwing at cocks, a day for football, rowdiness, and rebellion. And it is pleasing to find that it is still a special day for children in some parts of England, where 'Pancake Day', as they call it, is kept as a school holiday.

A 13-year-old girl writes:

'My special day is Pancake Day, every child has a holiday. Sometimes a fair comes to Longton and I think that everyone goes. Some children make up rhymes about pancake day such as –

Pancake Tuesday, mother's busy baking,
We are helping, lovely pancakes making,
Pancake Tuesday, mix them up and fry them,
When they are done you can come and try them.'

A 14-year old girl writes:

'A day that I always remember is Shrove Tuesday. On this day as we all know we have pancakes. We have the whole day off from school and the thing I remember about it is that all the children sing –

Pancake day is a very happy day,
If we don't have a holiday we'll all run away,
Where shall we run, up High Lane,
And here comes the teacher with a great big cane.

All the streets are crowded with children, running, skipping, and jumping.'

At Toddington in Bedfordshire when the traditional Pancake Bell is rung at twelve noon, the children rush out of school, as they have done for generations, and flock to Conver Hill to put their ears to the ground to hear 'the Old Woman frying her pancakes' underneath.

At Scarborough where a Pancake Bell is also rung (as at many other places), the special joy to the young, and even to the not so young, is the mass-skipping on the Foreshore, an exercise which has been traditional at Scarborough on Shrove Tuesday for 200 years. By the afternoon, even in frosty or snowy weather, the Foreshore is alive with skippers and the roadway becomes utterly blocked to traffic. Townsmen and people from the surrounding villages bring great lengths of clothes-line with them, and skip ten and even fifteen abreast in each rope.

Away in the West Country children still sing:

Tippety, tippety tin,
Give me a pancake and I will come in.
Tippety, tippety toe,
Give me a pancake and I will go.

'If your doors are left open,' writes a correspondent, 'the children with blackened faces will creep in and throw a load of broken crocks all over the floor and try to leave unseen. If the householders chase and catch them they further black their faces with soot, and then give them a cake before letting them go.'

C   Kissing Friday

A teacher writing to the *Yorkshire Post* tells how after Ash Wednesday, comes Kissing Friday. A few years before, when she arrived at a country school and was taking a mixed class of 13-year-old children in country dancing, she saw the leading boy suddenly lean across and kiss his partner, who showed no sign of embarrassment. When, as teacher, she expressed her surprise, the boy said, 'It's all right, Miss. You see, it's Kissing Friday', and explained that on Friday following Shrove Tuesday any lad had the right to kiss any girl without being resisted.

'And so it proved. For at each break in lessons every girl was soundly kissed by any boy she encountered. It was useless for me to expostulate, so I did not try. But each year as Kissing Friday came round, the school was in turmoil.'

A correspondent to the same paper recalled that when he was a boy he and his fellows used to pinch each other's ears. A Yorkshireman broadcasting in January 1955 recalled that, when a boy, on Kissing Day, the boys would challenge all comers, their girl friends in particular, by putting a rope across the road on the way to school and demanding either a kiss or a forfeit.

Reading Games, © Jill Hadfield and Charles Hadfield 1995

April Fool's Day

The first day of April ranks amongst the most joyous days in the juvenile calendar.

'It is a day when you hoax friends of yours with jokes like sending them to the shop for some pigeon's milk, or telling them to dig a hole because the dog has died; when they come back and ask where is the dead dog you say "April fool" and laugh at them.

Teachers come in for their share of the fooling, and according to a 12-year-old girl are the most exciting prey:

'The best joke I ever saw was in school when one of our girls brought another girl dressed as our new needlework mistress into the form room. She was introduced to the mistress who was taking us, and she was completely taken in. She even told us to stop laughing at the new mistress. Then we shouted "April Fool" to her and we all had a good laugh.'

And parents, of course, are not exempt. 'We have a lovely time,' says an 11-year-old Swansea girl, 'as there are so many jokes to play such as sewing up the bottom of Daddy's trousers.' And a 9-year-old Birmingham boy writes:

'Last year I fooled father by glue-ing a penny to the floor and saying "Dad you've dropped a penny on the floor." He couldn't get it off the ground because it was stuck firm, then I shouted "Yah, April Fool".'

In Scotland the day is generally known as 'Huntigowk Day'. Thus a 12-year-old girl in Edinburgh writes:

'Huntigowk is a day I love. I like to put a basin of water at the side of my sister's bed and hear her let out a yell when she puts her feet into it. I also put an empty eggshell in an eggcup so that when she opens it she finds that there is nothing inside it. I played a joke on my aunt once. She has a good sense of humour and can take any kind of a joke. When the butcher rang for the order I told my aunt that it was her boy-friend (my aunt is only in her twenties). So she rushed to the telephone and asked where he would meet her tonight. She did get a fright when the man said,

"Madam! What is the order for the butcher?"
"I'll go and ask," she stuttered, and when she walked into the kitchen to ask my mother I shouted "Huntigowk!"'

May Day: *1 May*

On the first of May, in country districts, young maidens rise early and go out into the dawn, as they have done for centuries, to wash their faces in the May dew. In Somerset children call this 'kissing the dew'. In most places, the girls do so to ensure that they shall have a beautiful complexion for the rest of the year. In some places the girls pat the dew on their faces to rid themselves of pimples. In others the dew is thought a certain cure for freckles. A 13–year-old girl states that the rite is customary there because it is said to bring luck. And an 11-year-old says that it is believed that if, on the first of May, a girl washes her face in the morning dew she will marry the first man she meets thereafter.

The traditional custom of shouldering little maypoles round the streets or visiting houses with may-garlands is still practised in some districts.

A teacher writes from near Oxford:

'I have made enquiries among my children in school and I find that ... little groups are formed and a May Queen is chosen. A small maypole is made and decorated with a garland a-top, and the Queen carries a stool upon which she sits for the ceremony, which is performed at intervals along the streets. She, by the way, wears a lace curtain and a ring on her finger, if possible. The rest of the company dance round her singing:

Round and round the maypole
Merrily we go,
Tripping, tripping lightly
Singing as we go.

O, the happy pastime
On the village green,
Dancing in the sunshine –
Hurrah for the Queen!

Here they all kneel on one knee and the Queen stands up and sings:

I'm the Queen, don't you see,
Just come from the meadow green;
If you wait a little while
I will dance you the maypole style.

My hair is long, my dress is short,
My shoes are laced with silver,
A red rosette upon my breast
And a guinea gold ring on my finger.

Then all the company rises and, oddly enough, begins to hop round the maypole singing:

Hop, hop, hop, to the butcher's shop,
I dare not stay any longer,
For if I do my ma will say
You naughty girl to disobey.'

F Halloween: *31 October*

Many children attend Hallowe'en parties. 'The best thing about the party,' says one girl, 'is that you should go in fancy dress. The most popular dress is a Witch's outfit, or something to do with lucky charms. It is said that one of the luckiest things at a Hallowe'en party is for a person to come in with a lump of coal.'

The games traditionally played at Hallowe'en are mostly peculiar to this night.

Duck Apple. A large bowl or tub is filled with cold water (sometimes soapy water) and a number of apples floated in it. One or two players at a time get down on their knees and, with their hands behind their backs (not infrequently with their hands tied behind their backs), try to get hold of one of the apples with their teeth. 'When they have done this they must lift the apple out of the basin. If they do this they may eat it.'

'If you take a bite of the apple nothing will happen to you, but,' exults an 11-year-old, 'if you miss, your head goes into the water with a splash.'

Forking for Apples. This is similar to Duck Apple but when the player's hands have been tied behind his back a fork is placed between his teeth. He has to kneel on or lean over a chair beside the tub, and must try to stab one of the floating apples and lift it out.

Bob Apple is also known as 'Snap Apple', or 'Apple on the Line'. 'First of all some sort of hook or nail must be available over a doorway. An apple is cored and the end of a length of string about a yard long is tied through the centre of the apple. The other end of the string is tied to the hook or nail. The string is twisted and the apple is sent spinning round on the end of the string, and people in turn try to catch the apple with their mouths and eat as big a mouthful as they can.'

Hallowe'en is the night above all others when supernatural influences prevail.

'At Midnight,' says a 14-year-old in Aberdeen, 'all the girls line up in front of a mirror. One by one each girl brushes her hair three times. While she is doing this the man who is to be her husband is supposed to look over her shoulder. If this happens the girl will be married within a year.'

'After they have done this,' continues the young Aberdonian, 'each girl peels an apple, the peel must be in one piece, then she throws the peel over her left shoulder with her right hand. This is supposed to form the initial of her husband-to-be.'

Nuts are also in requisition. 'A person has to place two nuts side by side near the fire,' says a Golspie boy. 'One represents oneself and the other stands for the person one hopes to marry. If the nuts, when they catch fire, burn quietly beside each other, the two will be married; if they burn vigorously and jump apart, the two will have a row and part.'

G Mischief Night: *4 November*

From coast to coast across northern England the 4 November has become 'Mischief Night', a night of humour and hooliganism. On this night children are half under the impression that lawlessness is permissible. Householders' front doors are repeatedly assaulted with bogus calls, their gates removed, their dustbin lids hoisted up lamp posts, their window panes daubed with paint, their doorknobs coated with treacle, their evening newspapers (projecting from letter-boxes) exchanged, their milk bottles placed so that they will be tripped over, their house-numbers unscrewed and fixed on to other houses, their windows tapped, their backyards turned upside down and possibly ransacked for tomorrow's bonfires, their drainpipes stuffed with paper and set alight. Both in villages and in great cities youngsters bent on mischief roam the streets in happy warfare with the adult world.

'On Mischief Night,' writes a 12-year-old, 'my friends and I do many strange mischievous deeds. We knock at a door offering a woman cabbages, meanwhile somebody climbs on the roof with a bucket of water. If the person will not buy she gets wet through.'

'On Mischievous Night,' writes another, 'one of our tricks is to collect some old tin cans, and tie them together with string. Then we fill them with ashes, tie a loop at the other end of the string, and put that on a door knob. Somebody knocks on the door and everybody hides. When the door is opened in flies the ashes, and then all sorts of language is heard.'

'A favourite trick,' say several lads, 'is to tie two door knobs together with a length of string, and knock at both doors at the same time.' The boys run and hide in a place where they can see both doors, and 'watch the occupants tugging against each other'. Sometimes, as the householders tug more and more strenuously, they creep out of their hiding places and cut the string, 'and both people' – so they hope – 'fly backwards as the doors fly open'. Alternatively, says a 12-year-old, 'a rope is tied to a door handle, and one of the boys knocks on the door. Some more boys hold the rope firmly, and when the man or woman attempts to open the door he cannot. Only when he pulls with all his strength do the boys let go of the rope. The man falls flat on his back.'

H New Year's Eve: *31 December*

In Wales and in the north of Britain almost all children are allowed to stay up until midnight, or are woken up then, so that they can watch the customs which let the Old Year out and bring the New Year in. Just before midnight, the ashes are cleared from the fireplace so that the year will be begun afresh. In several places, both the front door and the back door are opened to assist the Old Year's departure and the arrival of the New. Money, especially silver money, is placed outside the door, and bread and a piece of coal are put out as well to ensure health, wealth, and happiness to the household when fetched in the next day. In many English homes, as well as Scottish, they await the first-footer who, when he arrives, is welcomed with the warmest hospitality. It is a good thing everywhere if he is a man 'tall, dark-haired, and handsome'. He should 'cross the threshold with wood, coal, and silver coins in his hands to ensure the well-being of the household for the coming year' (in some places). He should have 'a glass of wine in one hand and a lump of coal in the other'. In others, where he is known as the 'lucky bird', he should have a lump of coal and, if possible, a sprig of evergreen. 'A few minutes before twelve o'clock,' writes a 14-year-old Scots girl, 'all the doors of the houses are opened to allow the spirit of the old year to depart. Then the clock strikes twelve, the church bells ring, the siren of the local mill is sounded, and everyone wishes everyone else "A Guid New Year". Then toasts, kisses, handshakes, and usually "Auld Lang Syne" is sung. With the advent of the New Year groups of people go 'first-footing'' armed with black bun, their "bottle", and perhaps a piece of coal. It is essential that the first man to cross the threshold in the New Year is tall and dark, to bring luck to the household. The rest of the night is spent in eating, drinking, singing, and dancing.'

Fill in the calendar with the names of the festivals.

Calendar

	Festival	Activities/Customs
JANUARY		
FEBRUARY		
APRIL		
MAY		
OCTOBER		
NOVEMBER		
DECEMBER		

Write in the customs from this list in the right place on the calendar:

- people place money and bread outside the door
- girls put nuts in the fire
- girls wash their faces in the dew
- children visit houses with garlands of flowers
- children tell people things that aren't true
- girls brush their hair in front of the mirror
- children play duck apple
- people make and throw pancakes
- children ask for gifts
- everyone goes skipping
- boys can kiss any girl they like
- a bell is rung
- children play tricks on grown-ups
- girls throw apple peel over their shoulder
- householders welcome a tall dark man with wood, coal and silver coins

Reading Games, © Jill Hadfield and Charles Hadfield 1995

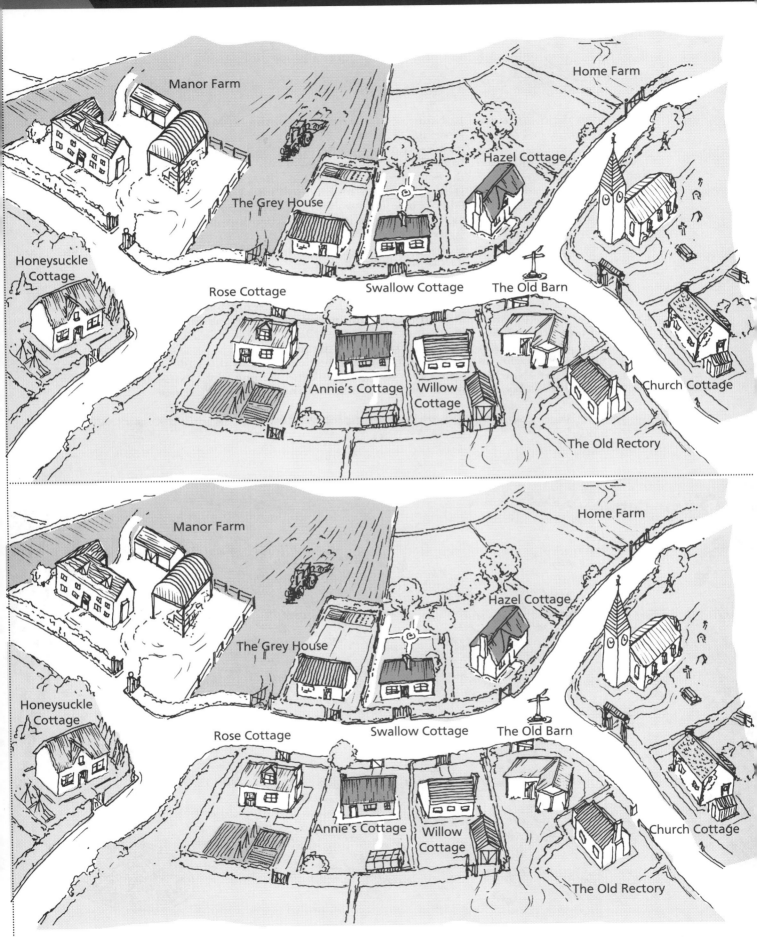

Manor Farm

Home Farm

The Grey House

Hazel Cottage

Honeysuckle Cottage

Rose Cottage

Swallow Cottage

The Old Barn

Annie's Cottage

Willow Cottage

Church Cottage

The Old Rectory

Manor Farm

Home Farm

The Grey House

Hazel Cottage

Honeysuckle Cottage

Rose Cottage

Swallow Cottage

The Old Barn

Annie's Cottage

Willow Cottage

Church Cottage

The Old Rectory

A Grey House — Cutting from the *South Hams Clarion*, 2 December 1926

Cutting from the *South Hams Clarion*, 2 December 1926

Combeford Police said last night that they were investigating a series of financial misdoings involving a number of prominent local businessmen. It is thought that the investigations are linked to the mystery surrounding the recent Torcliff Hotel robbery.

Mr Charles Robson, of Grey House, Combeford, was detained for questioning last night, and it is thought charges have been brought. He is to appear at Newton magistrates court today. Mr Robson has long been associated with the local hotel and restaurant trade, and from 1922-24 was chairman of the Southwestern Rotary Club. It is not known how many other people are involved, but at least five prominent local figures have been seen entering the police station in the last twenty-four hours.

Readers will recall that in June this year a series of break ins at local hotels culminated in the theft of cash and jewellery valuing £20,000 from the five star Torcliff Hotel. At the time police were unable to link the series of break ins, but in August Mr Charles Robson, who was managing director of the Torcliff, disappeared while on a business trip to France. Reappearing six weeks later, he claimed to have been kidnapped and that his brother William had been obliged to pay a ransom of £5000.

Mr William Robson is unavailable for comment, having been involved in a mysterious road accident on Dartmoor in November. He is still in a coma in Exeter Hospital, and police are hoping to interview him once he regains consciousness.

B Rose Cottage

Wednesday 6th May, 1926

A day I will never forget so long as I live. He smiled at me, so sweetly, with eyes so full of grace and love I thought I would melt in a pool of grateful tears at his feet. It was the Sunday School picnic outing, and I had of course volunteered to take charge of the sandwiches, and made arrangements with Joyce to meet at the village hall before the children asembled. The charabanc arrived in good time, and all the children were there, so sweet in their new clothes (little Rosey Baites a picture in that blue smocking dress). As luck would have it, both the class teachers and the headmistress had decided to accompany the outing, which left one place too few on the bus, and only one place to spare in the vicar's Austin! I could not believe my luck when the Reverend caught my eye, and asked if I needed a ride...though I must say I had carefully helped Mrs Hobbins into the bus after Mr Pyethwaite, and hoped I had calculated the number of places accurately.

He is so eloquent, so kind, so thoughtful, such a combination of spiritual wholesomeness with, dare I say it, masculinity. As we climbed the hill overlooking the river, the engine began to overheat, and we had to stop for a few minutes in the shade to let the engine cool (I say nothing of my fluttering heart!). We chatted, of this and that, and I refrained from asking more than 'Do you enjoy your new parish, vicar?' and the reply he gave made me blush : 'A beautiful parish such as this, is only enhanced by the beauty of certain of the parishioners, and at this time of the year who could ask for more?'

The picnic itself, of course, passed without event, and I was unable to prevent Mrs Ogwell from having a ride back to the village in the vicar's car But I shall see him again tomorrow, at choir practice, and, oh, hope I have not entirely mistaken the meaning of his words.

C Hazel cottage

School Report   *Mark Bainthorpe*   Form 6 Summer Term, 1926

<u>Geography:</u> *Shows a real local knowledge of the countryside, all without the benefit of maps. If he could keep his geographical explorations within the covers of his atlas and exercise book, he would make more progress.*

<u>Arithmetic:</u> *Numbers, at least those on the clockface, do not seem to be Mark's forte, and he would do well to add timekeeping to his range of hobbies, subtract idleness, and multiply his school hours by the common factor HARD WORK.*

<u>English:</u> *Mark's colourful use of the spoken language leaves little to be desired in its breadth of expression and precocious use of adult vocabulary. A pity such verbal dexterity is not reflected in his writing which has the inestimable value of great rarity.*

<u>Natural History:</u> Mark has the born countryman's instinctive knowledge of the land, and his skill in identifying the plants and birds and animals is unequalled. He should learn however that 'homework' means sitting at home with pen and paper, and cannot be interpreted as accompanying certain gentlemen on their forays onto private land under cover of darkness (though it must be said, the brace of pheasant were most welcome).
Practical work (e.g. at harvest time) is no doubt a useful preparation for a career in agriculture, nonetheless if this necessitates continued prolonged absences from lessons we will have to investigate Mark's future in the school rather more closely.

D Manor Farm Postcard from Bujumbura, Central Africa, dated 12 October 1926

My dearest sister Olive,

My heartfelt thanks for the parcel which arrived safely last week. You have no idea how much such tokens of friendship mean to us, as we labour for the Lord in this benighted yet beautiful land. As I write, the waters of Lake Tanganyika are ablaze with the sunset fires, and as the single bell of our lowly chapel rings for evensong, I cannot help but think of the peal of bells which used to echo (and still do I trust) around our green valley of Combeford, and the figures of the saints carved into those old oak pews. Think of me next time you are in St Andrew's, and pray for my flock of Africans. They sing so beautifully, and dance, and I truly believe they are numbered amongst the blessed (but it is hard work sometimes, especially now the rains are starting, and the risk of fevers and other ailments increases). I will send you shortly some examples of their weaving which is quite exquisite, and would not look out of place as a set of hassocks for St Andrew's. This may possibly reach you in time for Christmas.

Yours in trust and fellowship,

Peace Hooper

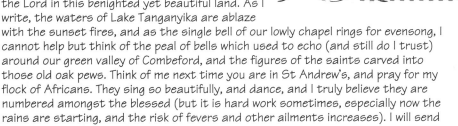

E Willow Cottage

Extract from the Parish Magazine: 11 November, 1826

And I commanded, and search hath been made, and it is found that this city of old time hath made insurrection against kings, and that rebellion and sedition have been made therein. (Ezra, 4:19)

Sadly, we have to report that in this parish of Combeford St Andrew's, last week two of our parishioners came to bloody combat of arms, and that one Douglas Algernon Fortescue Hoskin of Willow Cottage was slain by his fellow, Matthew Franklin Cooper, of The Old Barn Farm with a pistol ball which pierced his left lung and wounded him mortally. Duelling has been outlawed by Act of Parliament, yet still, it seems, our countrymen choose mortal combat over the law of the land as a means to settle disputes. We have all known Matthew, and Douglas, since they were infants baptized in our parish font. Two finer, more upstanding young men one could not hope to find the length and breadth of the county. And yet, all the education and Christian upbringing we have given them has come to naught. Douglas lies dead, and Matthew has fled for lands as yet unknown. We pray for them both, and wish their families comfort in these times of distress. Your prayers are requested for the poor woman Amy Sheldon of Church Cottage who came betwixt them:

'Thou shalt fear the LORD thy God, and serve him, and shalt swear by his name' (Deuteronomy, 6:13)

Extract from the Parish Magazine: November, 1926

On the second Thursday of November, Miss Hoskin gave a most interesting talk to the assembled ladies of the village on the subject of 'Ghosts: where do modern Christians stand?' It has long been a subject of dispute between the parishioners and the ministry, whether or not our beloved church of St Andrew is haunted by one or two ghosts, those of Crusaders killed during the Middle Ages. What brought Miss Hoskin's talk right up to date was the revelation that her own house, Willow Cottage, seems to be haunted too. On All Souls Day, just as she was hanging out the washing, Miss Hoskin distinctly felt a presence behind her in the garden. She turned, and glimpsed the figure of a young man smiling kindly at her. She spoke to the apparition, but without a word he smiled again, and seemed to aim a pistol into the air, before vanishing into the sunlight. Miss Hoskin wonders whether this new Combeford ghost is connected with the old tale of a duel in the village some one hundred years ago...

F Honeysuckle Cottage

TELEGRAM from Sam Harper, dated 12 May 1926, Cape Town.
On board SS WINDSOR CASTLE, London-bound from Sydney

Mrs Agatha Harper	Honeysuckle Cottage Combeford Devon

MOTHER AM ON WAY HOME STOP ARRIVE SOUTHAMPTON END MAY WILL COME DIRECTLY TO DEVON STOP HOPE YOU ARE WELL AND HETTY AND BETSY TOO STOP HAVE MISSED YOU ALL AND REGRET MY LONG SILENCE STOP FATHER WROTE BEFORE HE DIED SAYING GO WEST YOUNG MAN STOP INSTEAD I WENT EAST AND AM NO LONGER YOUNG BUT AM VERY RICH STOP I HAVE GREAT PLANS FOR YOU ALL AND HOPE YOU WILL BE FIT ENOUGH TO TRAVEL BACK WITH ME TO AUSTRALIA STOP THE WEATHER THERE IS MUCH KINDER FOR OLD PEOPLE STOP LOOKING FORWARD TO SEEING YOU AGAIN AFTER A LONG DECADE STOP LOVE YOUR SON SAMUEL

G Annie's Cottage

Swallow Cottage,
Combeford

3 June 1926

My Darling May,

How I long to hold you in my arms again, I cannot prevent myself thinking of you night and day, I sleep fitfully wondering whether you will keep your word and come to me.

How does your father treat you? Oh, I hardly dare think back to my mistake in ever approaching him. The cruel, the hard hearted (he is your dear father, true, but still I cannot bear the thought he still has control over your fate). To prevent our marriage! How dare he! He little knows the means I have at my disposal, and the look on his face when he realizes you have escaped him I would give my right arm to witness!

But patience. A week more, and we will be together. I am making the last arrangements and will send word via Anna, or failing that the gardener, Hoskin. I shall meet one of them at the market on Saturday, and they will tell you the details of my plan. But married we shall be, this side of Midsummer day, either in Gretna Green or over the sea in France.

Do not forget I love you, ever, and keep you in my heart as you do me.

Your true

Rodney

10 June 1926
Annie's Cottage,
Combeford

My dear Rodney,

Your letter is in my hand as I sit at the open window this beautiful summer evening. Tonight you will wait at Newton, and I will not come. You will think I have deceived you. No, never believe I will forget you, I love you so, and it is only the depth of my feeling that holds me here at home while you suffer such disappointments. But it is for the better, I would not have your name dragged through the mire of scandal and gossip, all for me, a poor hopeless girl who would be your ruin if you only knew how unworthy I am of you.

Rodney, do not regret my decision. It is for the best.

Courage, mon amour, je t'embrasse,

Your dearest May

H Home Farm

Tuesday 10 April, 1926

Dear Mrs Hooper,

Sorry to trouble you once again, but I wonder if I could ask you a favour, my Arthur being out of sorts and still refusing to speak a word to me.

He won't listen to me, so when he next comes to see to the sheep could you turn the conversation to our Mary's wedding? The date is fixed, for Midsummers Day, and we must go to the Rectory to speak with the vicar, to say nothing of arranging the wedding breakfast and engaging the musicians. I don't know what arrangements Arthur has already made, for he only ever talks to Mary, and now she's away in Plymouth. I must start sending the invitations myself. I need to know who Arthur is thinking of inviting, and whether for lunch or tea after the ceremony.

Also, could you tell him to order some green paint for the windows and woodwork next time he's at Newton market, as we want to get everything repainted in time.

Thanking you once again!

Your neighbour,

Gwen Bradninch

Tues 20 April, 1926

Dear Mrs Hooper,

Sorry to trouble you once again, but Gwen has decided not to speak to me it seems and I know she listens to you if no one else.

When she next comes to see you, could you turn the conversation to our Mary's wedding? The date is fixed, for Midsummers Day, and we must go and have a word with the vicar, to say nothing of arranging the wedding party and hiring a band of musicians. I don't know what plans Gwen has already made, for she only ever talks to Mary, (and now she's away working in Plymouth I'll have to start arranging things on my own). I need to know who Gwen and Mary are thinking of inviting.

Also, could you please ask her to order some green paint (one gallon of undercoat, one gallon of top coat gloss, Emerald Green) for the windows and woodwork next time she goes into Newton (Raleigh's the ironmongers on Queen Street), as I must get the house repainted in time for the wedding.

So sorry to trouble you, once again!

Your neighbour,

Arthur Bradninch

Where did these people live? Mark a—k on the village map.

a   a businessman who was arrested for fraud

b   an elderly lady who was in love with the vicar

c   two lovers who weren't allowed to marry

d   a naughty little boy

e   the vicar

f   a woman who became a missionary

g   a couple who lived in the same house but never spoke to each other

h   two men who fought a duel over a woman

i   the woman they fought over

j   a man who ran away to sea and then became a millionaire

k   the ghost of a young man

Where did these people live? Mark a—k on the village map.

a   a businessman who was arrested for fraud

b   an elderly lady who was in love with the vicar

c   two lovers who weren't allowed to marry

d   a naughty little boy

e   the vicar

f   a woman who became a missionary

g   a couple who lived in the same house but never spoke to each other

h   two men who fought a duel over a woman

i   the woman they fought over

j   a man who ran away to sea and then became a millionaire

k   the ghost of a young man

Where did these people live? Mark a—k on the village map.

a   a businessman who was arrested for fraud

b   an elderly lady who was in love with the vicar

c   two lovers who weren't allowed to marry

d   a naughty little boy

e   the vicar

f   a woman who became a missionary

g   a couple who lived in the same house but never spoke to each other

h   two men who fought a duel over a woman

i   the woman they fought over

j   a man who ran away to sea and then became a millionaire

k   the ghost of a young man

Where did these people live? Mark a—k on the village map.

a   a businessman who was arrested for fraud

b   an elderly lady who was in love with the vicar

c   two lovers who weren't allowed to marry

d   a naughty little boy

e   the vicar

f   a woman who became a missionary

g   a couple who lived in the same house but never spoke to each other

h   two men who fought a duel over a woman

i   the woman they fought over

j   a man who ran away to sea and then became a millionaire

k   the ghost of a young man

A

I usually wake about six and get immediately out of bed. Then I begin to wonder why. I have a fiendish attachment to something called Rose Geranium from Floris so I take a shower with a cloth which is green with the stuff – it's so aromatic that people down the street know that I've taken a shower and somehow I feel I've been pretty good to myself. I make very strong coffee and sit in the sunroom with the newspaper, the *Winston Salem Journal*, the only paper in town.

I love to read the letters to the editor. I like to see what angers people; only one in a hundred says 'I love what you're doing', the other 99 say they hate the paper or this is nonsense or that is absolutely wrong. I feel as if I've just met eight people, little human vignettes. And I look outside, I spend a lot of time looking outside. I live in a wooded area and I don't think, I just look.

At about 8.30 I start looking at the house because the housekeeper arrives at nine and I'm still too well brought-up to offer Mrs Cunningham a house in too much disarray so I straighten up before she comes in. She has been my housekeeper for six years now – my sister has suggested that in another life she was a staff-sergeant. I give to her and she gives to me and we live together with a lot of laughter. My secretary, Mrs Garris, also comes at nine and that's when real life begins. Mrs Garris is a lovely southern black lady with efficiency and grace vying for dominance in her spirit. She says, 'you've got to sign this, send that, agree to that, deny this ...' and I say, 'Mrs Garris, I will talk to you in an hour'.

At 10 I deal with my correspondence; I get about 300 letters a week. People send me all sorts of things, especially manuscripts. It's not fair, everybody's work deserves the attention of a qualified editor and I'm not that, so Mrs Garris writes back to explain that and to say that I don't read unsolicited manuscripts. Then she goes off to lunch and I usually invite friends over. I'm a very serious cook and I prepare what to me is a fabulous lunch for two or three people like breadcrumbed turkey-breast cooked in butter, wine and lemon, served with rice and zucchini and there's my home-made bread. I offer good wine and we laugh and talk.

B

At the time I suppose is tea-time for other people, I help myself to a very nice drink – Dewar's White Label whisky – and I look at my paintings. I'm a collector of black American art and I have paintings throughout my house, wonderful paintings that sing. It's a big house and I keep extending it. I always use the same builder and he says he's waiting for me to stretch down to the next street just to give me more walls for the paintings.

About seven I start to prepare dinner for myself; I drink more than I eat, but I prepare a proper dinner and put on candles and pretty music – all for me. If I'm not good to myself, how can I expect anyone else to be good to me? Then I read again, unless there's something on the television. Often something meaningless – sometimes I just don't want to be informed, increased, elevated, developed, I want something like an old Hollywood musical.

If I do go out I like to go to friends – however, unless there is an issue which calls for immediate discussion, I don't like cocktail chit-chat over Israel, or the Arabs. I think everyone young should do that with lots of cheap wine, sitting on the floor and shouting and arguing, but I don't do it now.

The issues have too much importance to be minimalised by someone saying, 'Now, where is Syria?' I love good stories, funny stories, told by the person against him or herself. That's what I want of an evening, then I go home to bed by 12.

When I'm writing, none of anything I've said applies. When I'm writing, everything shuts down. I get up at about five, take a shower and don't use the Floris – I don't want that sensual gratification. I get in my car and drive off to a hotel room; I can't write in my house, I take a hotel room and ask them to take everything off the walls so there's me, the Bible, Roget's Thesaurus and some good, dry sherry and I'm at work by 6.30. I write on the bed lying down – one elbow is darker than the other, really black from leaning on it – and I write in longhand on yellow pads. Once into it, all disbelief is suspended, it's beautiful. I hate to go, but I've set for myself 12.30 as the time to leave, because after that it's an indulgence, it becomes stuff I'm going to edit out anyway.

Then back home, shower, fresh clothes, and I go shopping for nice food and pretend to be sane. After dinner I re-read what I've written ... all that pretty stuff I've written gets axed out. So if I've written 10 or 12 pages in six hours, it'll end up as three or four if I'm lucky.

But writing really is my life. Thinking about it when I'm not doing it is terribly painful but when I'm doing it ... it's a lot like if I was a long-distance swimmer and had to jump into a pool covered with ice: it sounds terrible, but once in it and two or three laps done, I'm home and free ...

C

Wherever I am, I wake up around eight o'clock. I do not have an alarm or wake-up call. Breakfast is coffee and a croissant. Then I shower and put on make-up: some blue round my eyes and a bit of lipstick. For me it is important to feel good and look good.

If I am at home I am out riding by nine. I ride all day. You have got to practise, practise, practise. I have 15 horses, but I only take seven with me when I'm fighting.

I spent 10 years learning how to ride and kill bulls before I was good enough for the ring. Now I'm taken seriously because I fight well, not because I'm a woman. I regard myself as just another bullfighter. I don't want to take advantage of being female.

Fighting bulls on horseback makes men and women equal, which is not the case on foot, where women have to be manly. Anyway, the bullfighter's outfit does not flatter female contours and there is nothing feminine about a woman, covered in blood and sand, fighting a bull on foot.

I love everything to do with being a woman, even though I do a man's job in a very macho world. I can handle the macho bit. The problems come from the responsibility of knowing it is all down to me. My worst moments are when I am faced with a hard bull and I am not doing well, or when I am training on my own in the cold and rain. It is not all glory. The nervous stress brings tears on occasions.

My parents are proud of me now but when I told them I wanted to be a bullfighter they were shocked. Fortunately they never stood in my way. I think they reasoned that it was better to have a daughter with a head full of foolish ideas than no ideas at all. But, as the Spanish say, I was born for this.

I need to make £50,000 a year to pay for the horses and the rest of my team.

I have fallen off a lot and I have been tossed at least 10 times. The worst I have suffered is broken ribs. Of course it is dangerous. The bull is there to kill you. He doesn't think it's a game. When the bull gets you, it happens so quickly that you hardly have time to react. You just know you have to get up and save yourself.

D

At home I enjoy cooking, but when I'm travelling, I eat the regional food. If I am near the sea, I eat fish; if I'm inland, I like lamb.

I am very, very superstitious. I was superstitious as a little girl but I am more so now. I will not put a hat on a bed. You only do that when someone dies. When I leave my room, I leave the light on and expect to see it still burning when I get back.

I dress in a certain order. First, I touch up my make-up, then I put on my breeches, my blouse, the jacket, and then I polish my boots. When I am dressed, my friend Annie puts my hair up in a pony tail. Inside my blouse, dangling round my neck are five charms of La Vírgen del Rocío and La Macarena.

I am scared, not so much of being hurt, more of failure and criticism. Criticism hurts more than a fall. Some days, to do well, I take risks I would not otherwise consider. I know I risk my life but I don't like to talk about it. So far I have never thought I was going to die. If I ever have children, I'll stop. It is not fair to take these risks if others depend on you. The day I stop will be the day I wake and think: I've had enough; that's it.

During the season I see very little of Simon. Our paths do cross. My friends are the people I travel with. I don't have hobbies. I don't take holidays. Maybe in the winter, when I am not fighting, I'll go to Paris to do some shopping. There is a lot of administration involved, such as making sure people get paid, or the logistics of constantly being on the move, or last-minute changes and calamities to be sorted. I have to be a businesswoman as well.

A glass or two of red wine calms me down, especially before I go to bed. On the road, evenings usually consist of supper with my team. I eat something off the menu. I'm in bed, hopefully asleep, by midnight. I'm a light sleeper and I have recurring nightmares. One is that the horses aren't there. The most awful one is a bull that chases me into the car, back to the hotel, and there's nothing I can do to stop it, until I wake up with a start.

© Jill Hadfield and Charles Hadfield 1995

A typical day starts at 6 a.m. and I'll have 10 minutes longer in bed while Bill shaves. We have a television in the bedroom and I watch the business news on the BBC. Sometimes I feel quite exhausted and think, 'Oh Lord, wouldn't it be nice just to lie here for another hour or two,' but once I'm up I'm fine.

We go straight out to feed the horses and muck them out. There's no point in having a bath if you're out doing dirty work all day. I don't even make a cup of tea. We normally get back in about 7.30 and then there's the dog and two cats to feed while Bill will start making arrangements for his day.

Then we think about ourselves. I like a cooked breakfast, but when I'm racing I try not to eat much so I'll just have cereal and fruit. My average weight is around 9st 9lbs and Bill is about the same. Sometimes he's even lighter, which is very irritating and another incentive not to eat much. He's 37 and he encourages me to go on and that keeps me feeling younger. Over breakfast I read yesterday's papers, because today's haven't arrived yet.

Magnus needs plenty of exercise and hard work and that's not always easy as we don't have a lot of land. The horses go out six mornings out of seven, and at least once a week we ride them on Dartmoor. My helper, comes round at about 8.30 and we get the horses ready. Bill tries to arrange his work so that he can come.

As soon as we back, around 11, Bill goes off on his calls and Trudy and I brush the horses and give them any treatment they need. By the time that's finished and we've brought the two younger horses in, and given all of them their meal and cleaned up the tack and tidied the place up, it's at least one o'clock. Trudy goes home and I get some lunch.

Usually I have soup and bread and cheese, with perhaps a beer or a glass of red wine, but that's more likely in the evening.

In the afternoon I do my work as the secretary for the practice. I enter my husband's work from the previous day on the computer, type out letters and send out invoices. Bad debts have become rather a problem: one chap left the country last year owing us £1000. I've got tougher about it now and I chase people up on the phone because that's a lot more effective. I tell them that if they don't pay up I shall take legal action.

After a couple of hours I generally go into Okehampton to bank any cheques that have arrived, post letters and do a little shopping. When I get back I have to walk the dog. She expects it and it helps to keep me fit. I hate running so I walk as fast as I can, either up the hills or in the woods near our house. At this time of year I'm not back till about 5.30 but in the darkness of winter it's nearer 4.30 and I love to sit down for half an hour and watch television.

Then there's another round of mucking out and feeding the horses. I get back about seven and it's only then that I think about supper. I'll generally make something from mince or chops with our own vegetables. I've just got time to have a bath while the vegetables are cooking. I'm afraid I don't do much to look after my skin; I sometimes remember to use a moisturising cream at night but I never use cosmetics. I sometimes look at other people and think: 'Gosh, wouldn't it be nice to be made up like that,' but I'm simply too lazy.

My husband will probably be back by this time and we'll have a drink and talk about the day. Most evening we eat between 8.30 and nine and then watch the news. I'll fall asleep and my husband will wake me at 9.30 and we'll go out and take a last look at the horses, and then we're ready for bed.

Basically there isn't any evening. I'm always pretty shattered by the time I get into bed. My head hits the pillow and the next thing I hear is the alarm ringing.

Fill in the information for your character.

Personal information

Name ....

Age ....

Sex ....

Job ....

Marital Status ....

Children ....

Daily Routine

Wake up ....

Get up ....

Breakfast ....

Morning activities ....

....

Lunch ....

Afternoon activities ....

....

Dinner ....

Evening activities ....

....

Hobbies and Interests ....

....

Likes and Dislikes ....

....

Five adjectives to describe your character?

....

....

....

....

....

Maya Angelou has been a prostitute, a conductor on the San Francisco street-cars, a singer and dancer, a poet and a civil rights worker. She is now Reynolds Professor of American Studies at Wake Forest University and a best-selling author around the world. Ms Angelou is 59 and lives alone in North Carolina.

Marie-Sara Bourseiller 28, is the world's only professional 'rejoneadora' –female horseback bullfighter. She became fully-fledged two and a half years ago in Nîmes, Provence, where she lives on a big ranch with the bullfight impresario and breeder Simon Casas.

Rosemary Henderson 51, entered the 1994 Grand National on her horse Fiddler's Pike, which she calls Magnus. She worked as a secretary in London and New York before running a stable in Gloucestershire. She rode her first winner in 1973. She lives with her husband Bill, who is an equine vet, and trains their four racehorses near Okehampton, Devon.

Reading Games, © Jill Hadfield and Charles Hadfield 1995

A headmaster of a boy's school explains 'Why I became a schoolboy cheat'.

I know I should have told the headmaster at the time. That was my real sin.

He had gone out of the study for some reason leaving me alone and in his absence I looked to see what was on his desk. In the middle was a small piece of paper on which was written the words 'English Essay Prize 1949: History is a string of biographies'.

A moral boy would have avoided looking at the title as soon as he saw the heading. I did not. The subject of the English Prize was kept a secret until the start of the exam so I could not resist reading it.

When the headmaster returned I was looking out of the window.

I should have told him what had happened then. It would have been so easy to say: 'I'm sorry but I saw the title for the English Essay Prize on your desk. You'll have to change it.'

The opportunity passed and I did not take it. I sat the exam the next day and I won. I told myself I should have won anyway, but that is not the point. I didn't set out to cheat, but it was still cheating nevertheless.

That was 38 years ago when I was 18. The fact that the details are so clear suggests that I feel very guilty about it. I have never told anyone about it before, nor have I tried to explain to myself why not.

The obvious explanation is that I could not admit I had seen the essay title without admitting that I had been looking at the things on his desk; a good example of how a little error can trap you in a more serious moral corner. But there must have been more behind it. I wanted that prize very badly.

I think that is the reason I have hidden from myself for so long. I needed that prize to beat my arch rival. He had already won the English Verse and History Prizes.

It would be unbearable if he managed to beat me again. The prize I chose, a large anthology of verse entitled *Poetry of the English speaking World* is still on my bookshelf. I have often used the book. Inside the cover it says 'English Essay 1949'.

B

A novelist asks 'How could I fail my little granddaughter?'

My daughter Amy has a very beautiful one-year-old daughter. Her appearance seems to me even more astonishing when I take a look at my own – ravaged by 83 years of Life's struggle.

One lovely day I was left alone with my granddaughter in charge of the Miracle. At one o'clock the baby was having a nap and I was enjoying my favourite snack, a banana, and listening to the radio. I bit into the banana – and somehow, four new and expensive false teeth broke loose and stabbed through my tongue. At the same time the lump of banana stuck in my throat and I could not succeed in extracting the teeth from my tongue, which was now gushing blood.

Just to compound this unnatural dilemma, my darling began crying from her cot demanding to be lifted, fed and played with. With the banana advancing down my throat it was a desperate moment. Why not telephone an ambulance? Because I couldn't speak, you fool.

All this time, my darling was howling frantically. I knew her face would be going blue while I choked on the banana. When I looked at my own face in the mirror, it was turning from purple to black. It was in these circumstances that the doorbell rang and I staggered to answer it.

A tall and handsome black man was standing in the doorway. Dreadlocks fell over the collar of his smart dark suit. 'I'm the Gas,' he introduced himself. I could only open my mouth as wide as I could and point. 'Ah,' he said and, without hesitation, put in a finger and thumb and pulled my tongue free. Then, with no sign of disgust, he held both his palms beneath my chin to receive my four teeth and the lump of banana.

He made me a cup of tea while I lifted Maryanne from her cot. Quickly comforted, happy and amused, she dabbled her fingers in my tears of relief and gratitude, and licked them off my cheeks.

C

A writer remembers 'The lies I told the gentleman caller'.

Some years ago my husband and I separated, and soon afterwards, I had a series of visits from gentlemen callers. They came to comfort me they said. I wasn't convinced. Mostly I wasn't very receptive, and they took their comfort elsewhere, for the world is full of deserted women. One of them refused to go however, and over the months that followed, I was amazed by his sheer tenacity. His name was John Harper. I only went out with him once. We had dinner, and he offered me 3 courses of comfort. When we left, I vaguely promised to get in touch. He sent me several bouquets of flowers and phoned daily.

He was so persistent that I began to hate him. I instructed my teenage daughters who were at home at the time to answer each phone-call. 'If it's John Harper say I'm out,' I would yell. He became a family joke, and we even made up songs about him.

Every time the telephone rang I would yell, 'If it's John Harper, I'm out.' The girls would yell it in company with me. And then, one day, the inevitable

happened. When the phone rang, both my daughters were out. I picked up the phone and I was trapped. To my surprise I felt sorry for him and found myself inviting him to supper. He was more surprised than I was. As soon as I put the phone down I regretted the invitation.

He arrived at eight, with a huge bunch of roses. I welcomed him while my daughters giggled uncontrollably. Somehow or other we made conversation over the drinks. He still insisted on comforting me. It was a relief when we eventually sat down to supper.

Everything was fine until the dessert. I had just served the chocolate mousse when the phone rang. As soon as I heard the bell, like some Pavlovian dog, I automatically screamed across the table, 'If that's John Harper, I'm out.' Even the insistent ringing of the telephone could not disguise the silence that fell. My children fled from the room and left me alone with John Harper and the silence.

I decided that there was no way out, I had to tell him the whole truth, even though it would hurt him. He got up and left immediately and I never heard from him again.

Reading Games © Jill Hadfield and Charles Hadfield 1995

A journalist remembers 'My date with two girls.'

In 1969 I was working as a newspaper reporter and living in London, with someone I shall call Person A. One day in the office, my eye fell on a temporary secretary, whom I shall call Person B. Swaggering up to her desk I invited her out to lunch.

Over lunch she told me that she had been married but was now divorced and living at her parents' house. I leaned across the table. 'Can I see more of you,' I said. To which she replied, 'Well, I am completely free this weekend.'

Such an idea would normally have been impossible, but Person A was due to go into hospital that Thursday and stay there until the following Tuesday. The coast would thus be totally clear for me to entertain Person B in our flat for the whole weekend.

The only difficulty was the journey she must make to my flat from her parents' home. 'Just get a taxi', I told her grandly. 'I'll pay.'

On Friday I went to see Person A in hospital. 'I've got some great news,' she said. 'They said I can come home tomorrow.' 'Fantastic,' I said.

I walked very calmly from the ward, breaking into a run as soon as I was out of sight.

Clearly it was essential to contact Person B and stop her arriving. But how was I to find her? I didn't know her telephone number or address. I only knew that she was living with her parents.

Her surname was an unusual one. So I decided to look in the phone book until, with a sinking heart, I remembered she was a divorcee. Her name would be different from her parents. The phone book was no good. So I abused my position as a journalist.

I rang up the police in the area where Person B lived. I said I was a reporter investigating an important story, trying to find a young woman in that area. I asked the sergeant to go through the electoral register to see if there was anyone with Person B's surname.

The sergeant was extremely patient and searched painstakingly. But no one with Person B's surname was listed on the electoral roll.

By the next day the situation was desperate. In two hours the taxi cab would arrive in which I was to collect Person A from hospital. I still did not know how to cancel the taxi which was to deposit Person B outside my front door at around eight o'clock that night.

Then it occurred to me that as a temporary secretary Person B must be known to my paper's personnel department.

The personnel manager told me that the deputy was in charge of hiring temporary secretaries. With great helpfulness, he gave me the phone number of the deputy's cottage in Oxfordshire.

To the deputy personnel manager I told a dramatic tale of a temporary secretary taking home documents necessary for a front page story in the following day's paper.

'She must have been supplied to us by one of three agencies,' the deputy personnel manager said. 'I'll give you their numbers so you can ring them, but they may not be open on a Saturday ...'

My heart in my mouth, I dialled the first temp agency on the list. They did work on Saturday and they were the agency which had supplied Person B! They said they were sorry but couldn't give me her home telephone number but they would try to call her and ask her to ring me back. She rang 10 minutes before the taxi arrived to take me to hospital to collect Person A. I said we'd have to cancel our weekend because the paper was sending me abroad on a foreign assignment.

A cartoonist describes how she 'broke her foot on her husband's shin'.

My husband does not have many pleasant characteristics and on the night I kicked him he had none at all that I could see. I kicked him hard on the shin, an indication of my displeasure with his presence in the house. At the instant my bare foot made contact with the shin, I knew it had been A Bad Idea. I crumpled to the floor in pain and self pity, all my energy apparently having left me until I heard my husband say 'Stop pretending you've hurt your foot'.

All through eight years of marriage my husband has treated my problems as if I had invented them purely to ruin his social life. An illustration of his attitude is the occasion when we were sitting in a taxi on our way to the airport. I told him I felt sick and he only got halfway through saying 'I'm sure you're imagining it' when I threw up. So his reaction this time was no surprise.

I was unfortunately unable to kick him again so I hopped into the sitting-room and picked up a rather nice rosewood foot stool which I waved at him. I suppose the sight of a hopping wife waving a rosewood foot stool dangerously close to your head is just a little too much for anybody and he ran out of the house.

To my relief I was now on one side of the front door and he was on the other. I locked the door, hopped into the kitchen and consumed a big glass of brandy topped up with some cooking sherry. The effect was instant and I felt capable of attempting to crawl up two flights of stairs to bed.

As I crossed the hall I saw my husband peering through the letter flap. 'You're an awful actress,' he said.

Four hours later, I woke up in agony. I knew I needed medical help.

I managed to get down the stairs on my bottom and call a taxi which took me to hospital.

Six in the morning is a good time to have an accident as it turns out, because casualty is as quiet as a grave.

'How did you do it?' the doctor asked and I shamefacedly admitted I'd kicked my husband.

A week later I limped to a party and to my surprise there was a girl sitting at the other end of the room, also with her foot in plaster.

She had been visiting a friend of her ex-boyfriend who had considerately shown her a photograph of his new girlfriend. In her haste to get the picture under a brighter light and examine her rival the poor girl tripped and broke her toe.

So next time you see a woman with a limp you'll know a man was the cause.

A 1 Tick the emotions felt by the character in your anecdote.

   2 Put a cross by the emotions you feel, as you read the anecdote. Write in the reasons for feeling these emotions in the boxes, e.g. ANGER:I felt angry with him for deceiving his girlfriend.

B When you hear the other four anecdotes, tick the emotions felt by the character, and put a cross by those you feel as **you** listen to the story, in the appropriate box.

	Headmaster	Novelist	Writer	Journalist	Cartoonist
ANGER					
DISGUST					
HAPPINESS					
LAUGHTER					
DISLIKE					
ADMIRATION					
REGRET					
SHAME					
FEAR					
GUILT					
EMBARRASSMENT					
PAIN					
PANIC					
HUMILIATION					
RELIEF					
GRATITUDE					
IRRITATION					
HATE					
AFFECTION					
DISBELIEF					
SURPRISE					
DREAD					
DISCOMFORT					
ANTICIPATION					
LOVE					
WORRY					
DESPERATION					
SELF-PITY					
MISERY					

A

The Crow and the Pitcher

A poor crow, who was near to death with thirst, suddenly saw beneath her a water pitcher. Relieved and with great joy she flew swiftly down to it.

However, although the pitcher contained water, its level was so low that no matter how she stooped and strained she was unable to reach it.

Thereupon she tried to overturn the pitcher, hoping at least to drink from its spilled contents; but alas, it was too heavy for her.

At length, looking around, she saw some pebbles nearby. Picking them up, one by one, she dropped them into the pitcher. Slowly, by degrees, the water crept up to the very brim and she was at last able to quench her thirst.

It is easier to make a suggestion than to carry it out.

B

The Mice Meeting

Once upon a time a number of mice called a meeting to decide upon the best means of ridding themselves of a cat that had killed many of their relations.

Various plans were discussed and rejected, until at last a young mouse proposed that a bell should be hung round the tyrant's neck in future, so that they would have plenty of warning of her movements and therefore time to escape.

The suggestion was received joyfully by nearly all, but an old mouse, who had sat silently listening to the talk for some time, got up and said: 'While I consider the plan to be a very clever one, and feel sure that it would prove to be quite successful if carried out, I should like to know which brave mouse is going to put a bell on the cat?'

Necessity is the mother of invention.

The Ass and the Frogs

One day, a long time ago, a poor humble ass was making his way along a track with a load of wood upon his back. Suddenly, rounding a bend in the path, he came to a deep bog and, stumbling clumsily under his load, he slipped straight into it. Despite his frantic struggling, the ass had the bad luck to sink right up to his neck in the mud amidst a horde of leaping frogs.

'Woe is me!' he groaned and began to bray piteously; then he gave a long sigh as if his heart was about to break in two. The frogs leapt and splashed all round him as he settled deeper into the mire.

'Friend,' said one of the frogs to the unhappy ass, 'if you make such a fuss as this simply because you find yourself in a bog, what would you do if you lived here all the time, as we do?'

False confidence often leads to disaster.

The Ass, the Cock and the Lion

One day a great lion, feeling very hungry after many hours of fruitless hunting, decided to try and find a meal at a farm. He padded over towards the yard and there, as he expected, was a fine plump ass, foolishly munching and crunching at a briar.

The lion thought the ass would make an admirable meal, but perched on a nearby stile was a rangy old cock, and they say that there is nothing a lion hates so much as the crowing of a cock. The lion paused, then he took a step towards the ass, but at that moment the cock began to crow. The offended lion turned about and bounded off with all possible haste until he could no longer hear the awful noise.

The ass had idly watched these events and was highly amused at the thought of a lion being frightened by a cock, so he plucked up his courage and galloped after him, delighted to think that he, a mere ass, was chasing the king of the jungle.

However, the ass had not followed for long when the lion turned sharply round upon him. The unfortunate ass never had time to think about his error, and the lion was no longer hungry.

Custom makes things familiar and easy to us.

The Dove and the Ant

Through the forest ran a clear bubbling steam and under a blade of grass on the bank sat an ant. She felt very thirsty and bent over to take a drink, but as she did so she slipped and fell into the water.

The strong current snatched her away, carrying her far off down the steam. As hard as she tried she could not manage to swim to the bank.

At that moment a dove flew by and, seeing the struggling ant, took pity on her distress. She broke a branch from a nearby tree and dropped it into the water. The ant did not delay but clambered nimbly on to the branch and at last reached the safety of the bank.

Not long after this, the ant was out for a stroll when she came upon the dove again. A hunter was just about to trap the bird with a large net. Seeing what was going to happen, the ant bit sharply into the man's heel and made him cry out in surprise.

The dove heard him, took fright and flew away.

Misfortune tests the sincerity of friends.

The Travellers and the Bear

Two friends were travelling on the same road together when suddenly they came face to face with a large bear.

In great fear, and without a thought about his companion, one man immediately climbed into a tree and hid.

The other, seeing that single-handed he was no match for Bruin the bear, threw himself on the ground and pretended to be dead, for he had heard that a bear will not touch a dead body.

The bear approached him, sniffing at his nose and ears, but the man, with great courage, held his breath and kept still, and at length the bear, thinking him dead, walked slowly away.

When Bruin was well out of sight the first traveller came down from his tree and asked his companion what it was that the bear had said to him. 'For,' said he 'I observed from my perch that he put his mouth very close to your ear.'

'Why,' replied the other, 'it was no great secret. He wisely advised me not to keep company with those who, when they get into difficulty, leave their friends in the lurch.'

One good turn deserves another.

The Tortoise and the Eagle

A long while ago a tortoise sat on the dusty land and watched the birds wheeling and circling in the air over his head. He grew dissatisfied with his lowly life when he saw so many of them enjoying themselves in the clear blue sky; he longed to join them and share their freedom.

'If only I could get myself up into the air I'm sure I could soar and swoop with the best of them,' he thought.

He pondered on this problem for a long time: the sun burned down and he got hotter and hotter and more discontented as he enviously watched the birds.

Suddenly an eagle came to rest on a rock close beside him and, seizing such a favourable opportunity, the tortoise offered all the treasures of the sea if only the monarch of the air would teach him to fly.

The eagle at first declined the task, for he considered it not only absurd but impossible, but, being further pressed by the entreaties and promises of the tortoise, he finally agreed to try.

Taking him up to a great height in the air, the eagle loosed his hold, bidding the stupid tortoise to fly if he could.

Before the misguided creature could express a word of thanks he fell upon a huge rock and was dashed to pieces.

Don't count your chickens before they're hatched.

The Country Maid

A long a country lane stepped a bright young milkmaid, balancing a jug of fine fresh milk on her head. With a fair way still to go to reach the market she started thinking about her future prospects.

'If I sell this milk for a tidy price I can increase my stock of eggs to three hundred. Then, even allowing for those that spoil and those that are stolen by thieves, they should produce at least two hundred and fifty chickens. Then again, just when the price is highest, I will take the birds to market and sell them: I cannot fail to make enough money to buy a new gown. I am so fair and pretty I will look as grand as any lady in the land.'

'What colour should it be?' she thought. 'Shall I buy one in red or green? Yes, green, I think – it suits me best; green it will be! I'll go to the fair where all the fine young men will seek me out for a partner; but I shall refuse them, every one, and dance away with a shrug and a toss.'

Carried away by her daydream she could not help but toss her head in just such a way as she had imagined. Crash! The jug of milk toppled and smashed on to the road in front of her. She watched helplessly as the spilt milk trickled away in the dust, and with it went all of her happy thoughts and dreams.

The over-ambitious often destroy themselves.

Reading Games, © Jill Hadfield and Charles Hadfield 1995

I

The Miser's Gold

A very mean man once sold all his goods and property and melted the money he received for it into one solid mass of gold. He took the gold to a wood, where he buried it in the ground. He visited his hoard night and morning to gloat over it.

One night a robber spied on him and when the miser had gone the villain dug up the treasure and went off with it.

Next day the miser missed it and went nearly out of his mind at the loss of his gold. 'Why are you making such a noise?' said a neighbour. 'You might as well have a stone in the ground instead of your gold, for it was no use to you when you had it.'

Think for yourself, and don't follow the crowd.

J

The Sick Lion

An old, old lion realised one day that, thanks to the weakness of age, he was too tired to hunt for his prey any more. Sadly he went home to his den knowing that soon he would die. But before he lay down he stopped at the entrance; breathing with great difficulty and speaking in a slow, low voice he told the world of his sad condition. The news of the lion's illness soon spread throughout the forest and caused much concern among the other beasts. One by one they came to visit him and pay their respects. However, the lion's age had also made him wily, and as each animal entered his lair and came within reach, they fell an easy prey to the lion, who soon grew fat. One day, early in the morning, the fox came. He was renowned for his cunning, and approached the den carefully. Standing some distance away he enquired after the lion's health and asked him if he was feeling better.

'Ah, my dearest friend,' said the lion, 'is it you? I can hardly see you, you are so far away. Come closer, please, and give me some words of consolation for I have not long to live.'

The fox, meanwhile, had been looking closely at the ground in front of the lion's den. At last he looked up, and turning to go he remarked: 'Bless you, but excuse me if I do not stay, for, to tell the truth, I feel quite uneasy at the many footsteps I see leading into your den yet none do I see emerging.'

Riches are meant to be used.

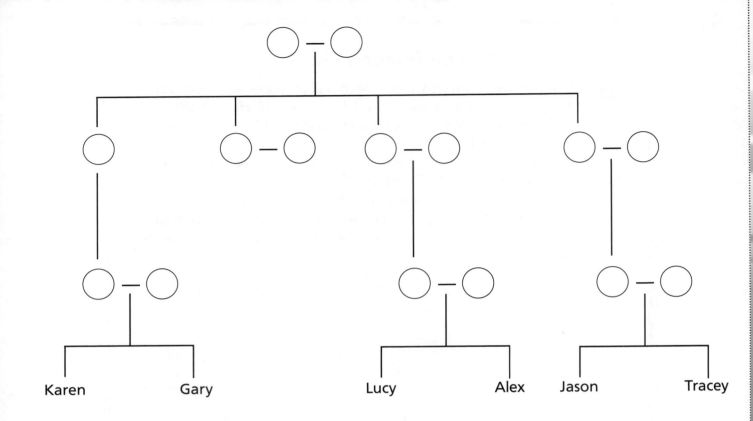

Karen   Gary   Lucy   Alex   Jason   Tracey

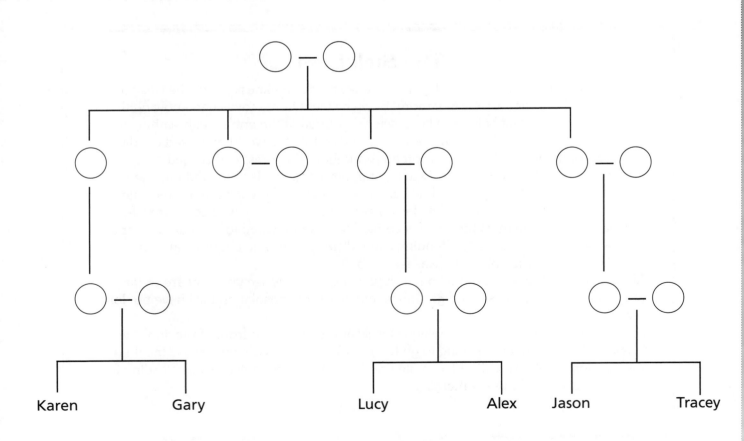

Karen   Gary   Lucy   Alex   Jason   Tracey

KAREN

You have a brother Gary and your parents' names are Jean and Hugh. You know your mother's maiden name was Clutterbuck and you think your grandmother's name was Maud – she's dead now. Your mother doesn't talk about her much and she never talks about your grandfather. You don't know anyone else in your family and wonder why you've never met.

GARY

You have a sister Karen and parents Jean and Hugh. You know your mother's maiden name was Clutterbuck and you think your grandmother's name was Maud – she's dead now. Your mother doesn't talk about her much and she never talks about your grandfather. You don't know anyone else in your family and wonder why you've never met.

LUCY

You have a brother, Alex . Your parents are Vera and Philip. That's all you know about your family though you think your mother's father was called Samuel.

ALEX

You have a sister Lucy . Your parents are Vera and Philip. That's all you know about your family though you think your mother's father was called Samuel.

TRACEY

You have a brother Jason. Your parents are Mike and Jane.Your grandparents are dead now, but you remember your father's father, Joseph, an old man with grey whiskers that tickled when he kissed you.

JASON

You have one sister Tracey. Your parents are Mike and Jane.
Your grandparents are dead now, but you remember your father's father, Joseph, an old man with grey whiskers that tickled when he kissed you.

THIS IS THE LAST WILL AND TESTAMENT OF LILY ALICE CATHERINE MARGARET CLUTTERBUCK of GLUMBY-in-SCARDALE, born on the eighteenth day of January 1890.

To JEAN ALICE , my granddaughter, only daughter of MAUD, I leave my entire estate, consisting of the house and garden , 100 acres of arable land, and the sheep grazing land, situated at Hillside, as well as the whole of possessions and money in my name after payment of funeral expenses and death duties, with the exception of the following:

To my daughter MAVIS, wife of William Thistlethwaite, I leave the Bedroom Mirror (the better for her to see the truth of her expression).

To my son SAMUEL, I leave the Soap Dish and Carbolic Soap to wash his mouth of the foul names he has called his brother.

To my younger son JOSEPH, I leave the old blackened Cookpot, that he should bethink himself in his quarrel with his brother, of the old saying, 'The pot should not call the kettle black.'

To HENRY my husband I leave the investments and bank accounts in trust the income from which is to cover the expenses of the Nursing Home until his death, at which time the remaining capital shall pass to the above-mentioned JEAN ALICE.

Signed

Lily Clutterbuck

Dated 8 December , 1949

A **Accompanying letter dated 8 December, 1949**

8th December, 1949

To My Family,

I am not long for this world, I know in my bones, despite what the doctors tell me. This is my last attempt to set the record straight and what you make of it is up to you. I'm tired of all your squabbling and bickering and if there's peace and quiet in the hereafter, then I'll be a happier woman when I leave you than I have since I first set eyes on your father.

You treated Maud wrong, the whole pack of you, and she died of heartache at the thought she'd lost the love of her own sister and her father and brothers. The poor girl did her best to raise an unwanted child. Jean, my granddaughter, will inherit all that I love and hold dearest, the farm and fellsides that were so dear to my parents, and she will have the goodness and strength of character to develop the land that none of you have ever cared for.

So the property will be a memorial to my dearest daughter Maud, who died alone and rejected, and her memory will erase the pettiness and meanness that have soured the rest of you. Henry is now so ill he won't know what I've done. He is as well cared for in the Nursing Home as he could be, and whether he lives another ten years or another ten weeks, it's all the same to him. I've loved him as well as I could, and I've tried, God knows, to raise a good family despite his behaviour.

The few possessions I leave you, are my final message to you. Samuel and Joseph – you have broken my heart with your foolish pride. I hope my gifts will teach you some humility. Mavis – you always thought yourself such a virtuous young lady. I hope you will look long and deep into the mirror and see yourself for what you really are. It may not be too late, even at your age, for you to learn some humility and respect.

And so I leave you, fully understanding what I am doing in making this last will and testament. Do not shed false tears for me, I am a happier woman now I can die with my mind at rest.

Lily

Pennine Bugle   *Tuesday, September 6, 1946*

PENNINE SHEEP SCANDAL; LOCAL MAN DETAINED FOR QUESTIONING.

UNDERCOVER LINKS WITH COUNTY REGIMENT

'We have uncovered a den of corruption and organized crime' say Police

Scardale 5 September, 1946

POLICE revealed yesterday that they have uncovered one of the most important sheeprustling networks in Northern England. Several arrests were made last week in the Scardale and Glumthorpe area, and three of those detained are now helping police with enquiries. Chief Superintendent Toyson issued a brief statement, stating that charges would be made today against three of the men, and that the persistence and hard work of Lancashire Constabulary over the past decade had led to the discovery of an agricultural crime network unprecedented in the history of the Pennines.

Our own investigations reveal that a local farmer Henry Clutterbuck, prominent among stockbreeders and market traders at Settle market and owning three hundred acres of fellside between Glumthorpe and Beckdale on the east side of the main Settle–Blackhole road, is among those currently detained at Glumby police station. It is alleged that over the past decade, taking advantage of meat rationing and increased demand for fresh meat, the farmer organized a widespread black market in meat, with the involvement of major slaughter houses on both sides of the Pennines. It is further alleged that the man's accomplice, a former sergeant major in the Pennine Borderers, was involved in undercover deals between the Ministry of Agriculture and Fisheries and the Ministry of Supply, revolving round the barracks at Carslisle.

Charges will be brought at Glumby magistrates court on Thursday...

10 August, 1951

Dear Mother,

I hope this letter finds you well now. I'm so glad you have recovered from the operation. I will try to come up to Hillside next weekend, or the weekend after, depending on how Joan is feeling. Little Vera is teething now and Joan is quite worn out. Things have not been easy lately I can tell you.

Now I know you wish me to forgive and forget, but I honestly don't know how you expect me to. I'll tell you about Joseph in a minute, but first things first. I was clearing up an old cupboard yesterday, and my eye happened to fall on this old copy of the 'Bugle' which was lining one of the drawers... so now I know what my own father is capable of! You know, you should not have tried to hide this scandal from me. I was away in North Africa and Italy for four years, fighting for my King and Country, and when I came out of the army in '47 and came back home I knew something fishy had happened.

But Mother, as you always told me when I was little, "The Truth will out like blossom after snow" and there's nothing will prevent folk finding out what happpened.

I'm writing you this so we can have a good talk and clear it all up when I visit next week.

Now as for Joseph, I don't know how you expect me to talk to him again when you haven't visited your own husband in his nursing home for the last five years! Joseph stole the woman I love. Do you expect me to forgive him? Elizabeth is the only woman I ever loved or ever will love. It is a daily torture for me to know she is married to Joseph. How could I bear to set eyes on either of them again? A son owes a duty to his mother, but please do not ask that of me.

Send me a note if you would like me to come to Hillside earlier.

Your son,

Samuel

Letter

'Moorlands'
Settle Road
Lowering-in-Grimsdale
W. Riding

29th February, 1952

Dear Mary,

Well spring has come to the fells — it's snowy and blowing up a storm and the lambs are on their way. Joseph is up all night with the sheep, and as there's no chance of a wink of sleep before dawn I thought I would catch up on my long overdue correspondence while sitting by the fire. I cannot sleep well these days since something is on my mind. Mary dear, I must tell you, since I must tell someone and I would not want to tell another living soul. Mary, I am pregnant and the child I am carrying is not Joseph's but his brother Samuel's. You know that once I was engaged to Samuel, but we broke after a quarrel and I married his brother. Well, I have never stopped loving him, nor he me. What is to be done? What an unhappy family we have become! The two brothers will not speak to each other, all on account of me, and Mavis will not speak to her sister Maud since she got herself in the family way and bore a child out of wedlock — jealousy I think since her own marriage is barren — and my mother in law Lily will not speak to her own husband since he had the stroke and went into the Nursing Home — no-one knows the reason why... Did you ever hear of such a quarrelsome family?

Well, does the snow come at lambing time in New Zealand too? I know so little of your new life, it sems so long ago that you and I would walk the lanes and the hillsides of the Pennines together. How our lives have changed since then — I hope at least yours is happier there than mine is here.

Your dear friend,

Elizabeth

On the Brighton Road

Slowly the sun had climbed up the hard white downs, till it broke upon a sparkling world of snow. Once above the sky-line, the sun seemed to climb more quickly, and as it rose higher it began to give out a heat that blended with the keenness of the wind.

It may have been this strange alternation of heat and cold that disturbed the tramp in his dreams, for he struggled for a moment with the snow that covered him, like a man who finds himself twisted uncomfortably in the bed-clothes, and then sat up with staring, questioning eyes. 'Lord! I thought I was in bed,' he said to himself as he took in the vacant landscape, 'and all the while I was out here.' He stretched his limbs, and, rising carefully to his feet, shook the snow off his body.

'Come, I feel pretty fit,' he thought. 'I suppose I am lucky to wake at all in this. Or unlucky – it isn't much of a business to come back to.' He looked up and saw the downs shining against the blue like the Alps on a picture-postcard. 'That means another forty miles or so, I suppose,' he continued grimly. The sun crept up higher and higher, and he started walking patiently along the road with his back turned to the hills.

Presently, when three milestones had loitered past, he overtook a boy who was stooping to light a cigarette. He wore no overcoat, and looked unspeakably fragile against the snow. 'Are you on the road, guv'nor?' asked the boy huskily as he passed.

'I think I am,' the tramp said.

'Oh! then I'll come a bit of the way with you if you don't walk too fast. It's a bit lonesome walking this time of day.' The tramp nodded his head, and the boy started limping along by his side.

'I'm eighteen,' he said causally. 'I bet you thought I was younger.'
'Fifteen, I'd have said.'
'Eighteen last August, and I've been on the road six years. I ran away from home five times when I was a little 'un, and the police took me back each time. Very good to me, the police was. Now I haven't got a home to run away from.'
'Nor have I,' the tramp said calmly.

'Oh, I can see what you are,' the boy panted; 'you're a gentleman come down. It's harder for you than for me.'
'I dropped by the roadside last night and slept where I fell. It's a wonder I didn't die,' the tramp said. The boy looked at him sharply.

'How do you know you didn't?' he said.
'I don't see it,' the tramp said, after a pause.

'I tell you,' the boy said hoarsely, 'people like us can't get away from this sort of thing if we want to. Always hungry and thirsty and dog-tired and walking all the time. And yet if any one offers me a nice home and work my stomach feels sick. Do I look strong? I know I'm little for my age, but I've been knocking about like this for six years, and do you think I'm not dead?

You'll find out presently. We're all dead, all of us who're on the road, and we're all tired, yet somehow we can't leave it. There's nice smells in the summer, dust and hay and the wind smack in your face on a hot day; and it's nice waking up in the wet grass on a fine morning. I don't know, I don't know –' he lurched forward suddenly, and the tramp caught him in his arms.

'I'm sick,' the boy whispered – 'sick.'

The tramp looked up and down the road, but he could see no houses or any sign of help. Yet even as he supported the boy doubtfully in the middle of the road a motor-car suddenly flashed in the middle distance, and came smoothly through the snow.

'What's the trouble?' said the driver quietly as he pulled up, 'I'm a doctor.' He looked at the boy keenly and listened to his strained breathing.
'Pneumonia,' he commented. 'I'll give him a lift to the infirmary, and you, too, if you like.'

The tramp thought of the workhouse and shook his head. 'I'd rather walk,' he said.

The boy winked faintly as they lifted him into the car.

'I'll meet you beyond Reigate,' he murmured to the tramp. 'You'll see.' And the car vanished along the white road.

The Clock

I was staying with my aunt in Hampstead. There was another guest, whom I had never met before, a Mrs Caleb. She lived in Lewes and had been staying with my aunt for about a fortnight. Frankly, I disliked her. She was queer and secretive; underground, if you can use the expression, rather than underhand. And I could feel in my body that she did not like me.

One summer day Mrs Caleb waylaid me in the hall, just as I was going out.

'I wonder,' she said, 'I wonder if you could do me a small favour. If you do have any time to spare in Lewes – only if you do – would you be so kind as to call at my house? I left a little travelling-clock there in the hurry of parting. If it's not in the drawing-room, it will be in my bedroom or in one of the maids' bedrooms. Would it be too much to ask? The house has been locked up for twelve days, but everything is in order. I have the keys here; the large one is for the garden gate, the small one for the front door.'

I could only accept, and she proceeded to tell me how I could find Ash Grove House.

'You will feel quite like a burglar,' she said. 'But mind, it's only if you have time to spare.'

I found Ash Grove without difficulty. It was a medium-sized red-brick house, standing by itself in a high walled garden that bounded a narrow lane. A flagged path led from the gate to the front door. The dining-room and drawing-room lay on either side of the hall and I looked round hurriedly for the clock. It was neither on the table nor mantelpiece. The rest of the furniture was carefully covered over with white dust-sheets. Then I went upstairs. I made a hurried search of the principal bedrooms. There was no sign of Mrs Caleb's clock. The impression that the house gave me – you know the sense of personality that a house conveys – was neither pleasing nor displeasing, but it was stuffy, stuffy from the absence of fresh air, with an additional stuffiness added, that seemed to come out from the hangings and quilts. The last door that I unlocked – (I should say that the doors of all the rooms were locked, and relocked by me after I had glanced inside them) – contained the object of my search. Mrs Caleb's travelling-clock was on the mantelpiece, ticking away merrily.

That was how I thought of it at first. And then for the first time I realised that there was something wrong. The clock had no business to be ticking. The house had been shut up for twelve days. No one had come in to air it or to light fires. And yet the clock was going. I wondered if some vibration had set the mechanism in motion, and pulled out my watch to see the time. It was five minutes to one. The clock on the mantelpiece said four minutes to one. I again looked round the room. Nothing was out of place. The only thing that might have called for remark was that there appeared to be a slight indentation on the pillow and the bed; but the mattress was a feather mattress, and you know how difficult it is to make them perfectly smooth. I gave a hurried glance under the bed and then, and much more reluctantly, opened the doors of two horribly capacious cupboards, both happily empty. By this time I really was frightened. The clock went ticking on. I had a horrible feeling that an alarm might go off at any moment, and the thought of being in that empty house was almost too much for me. However, I made an attempt to pull myself together. It might after all be a fourteen-day clock. If it were, then it would be almost run down. I could roughly find out how long the clock had been going by winding it up. I hesitated to put the matter to the test; but the uncertainty was too much for me. I took it out of its case and began to wind. I had scarcely turned the winding-screw twice when it stopped. The clock clearly was not running down; the hands had been set in motion probably only an hour or two before. I felt cold and faint and, going to the window, threw up the sash, letting in the sweet, live air of the garden. I knew now that the house was queer, horribly queer. Could someone be living in the house? Was someone else in the house now? I thought that I had been in all the rooms, but had I? I had only just opened the bathroom door, and I had certainly not opened any cupboards, except those in the room in which I was. Then, as I stood by the open window, wondering what I should do next and and feeling that I just couldn't go down that corridor into the darkened hall to fumble at the latch of the front door with I don't know what behind me, I heard a noise. It was very faint at first, and seemed to be coming from the stairs. It was a curious noise – not the noise of anyone climbing up the stairs, but of something hopping up the stairs, like a very big bird would hop. I heard it on the landing; it stopped. Then there was a curious scratching noise against one of the bedroom doors, the sort of noise you can make with the nail of your little finger scratching polished wood. Whatever it was, was coming slowly down the corridor, scratching at the doors as it went. I could stand it no longer.

All the morning the tramp splashed through the thawing snow, but at midday he begged some bread at a cottage door and crept into a lonely barn to eat it. It was warm in there, and after his meal he fell asleep among the hay. It was dark when he woke, and started trudging once more through the slushy roads.

Two miles beyond Reigate a figure, a fragile figure, slipped out of the darkness to meet him.

'On the road, guv'nor?' said a husky voice. 'Then I'll come a bit of the way with you if you don't walk too fast. It's a bit lonesome walking this time of day.'

'But the pneumonia!' cried the tramp aghast.

'I died at Crawley this morning,' said the boy.

Nightmare pictures of locked doors opening filled my brain. I took up the clock wrapped it in my mackintosh and dropped it out of the window on to a flower-bed. Then I managed to crawl out of the window and, getting a grip of the sill, 'successfully negotiated', as the journalists would say, 'a twelve-foot drop'. Picking up the mackintosh, I ran round to the front door and locked it. Then I felt I could breathe, but not until I was on the far side of the gate in the garden wall did I feel safe.

Then I remembered that the bedroom window was open. What was I to do? Wild horses wouldn't have dragged me into that house again unaccompanied. I made up my mind to go to the police-station and tell them everything. I had actually begun to walk down the lane in the direction of the town, when I chanced to look back at the house. The window that I had left open was shut.

No, my dear, I didn't see any face or anything dreadful like that … and of course, it may have shut by itself. It was an ordinary sash-window, and you know they are often difficult to keep open.

And the rest? Why, there's really nothing more to tell. I didn't even see Mrs Caleb again. She had had some sort of fainting fit just before lunch-time, my aunt informed me on my return, and had had to go to bed. Next morning I travelled down to Cornwall to join mother and the children. I thought I had forgotten all about it, but when three years later Uncle Charles suggested giving me a travelling-clock for a twenty-first birthday present, I was foolish enough to prefer the alternative that he offered, a collected edition of the works of Thomas Carlyle.

A What the butler saw

The dinner guests started arriving at about 7.30. That evening, Reverend Truelove, the neighbours, old Mr Archibald and his son, and Dame Christie, a lady novelist, were joining the weekend guests.

I served drinks in the parlour before dinner. From the start I could see things weren't going too well. Miss Daphne looked as if she had been crying, and after she had spoken a few words to young Mr Archibald in the hall, that young gentleman looked pretty unhappy too. Mr Jeffery looked extremely angry – he can look quite violent at times. The actress, Miss Topless, looked furious too, and I could see why: her companion, Mr Oscarsson had been flirting with Mrs Horsehair all weekend, and as I served the wine at dinner I noticed that they were having a particularly intimate conversation at one end of the table.

Dinner ended at about nine o'clock, and I served port to the gentlemen in the billiard room. As I left the kitchen, Miss Daphne came up to me, and, looking appealingly at me – she always looks so pretty in blue – pressed a note into my hand, asking me to give it to young Archibald.

I couldn't help reading the note, which said:

> Darling,
> Meet me in the conservatory at 9.30. I have a plan.
> Desperately,
> Daphne.

I served port in the billiard room, and passed the note surreptitiously to young Mr Archibald. Then I went back to the kitchen where I remained until shortly after half past nine, when I went back into the billiard room to refill the port glasses. As I was crossing the hall, Miss Topless came out of the parlour and went over to the ballroom. As she opened the door, I heard voices, and caught a glimpse of a young man in a white suit. I'm sure it was Mr Oscarsson.

I went into the billiard room to find only old Mr Archibald, Reverend Truelove and Mr Jeffery. Mr Archibald took a glass of port and said he would join the ladies in the parlour, and the Reverend followed him. Mr Jeffery took the port decanter from me and went into the library, saying he had an urgent letter to write.

I returned to the kitchen and stayed there till about ten o'clock when I heard a piercing scream. I rushed into the hall and found Charlotte, the maid, standing there with a tray of coffee cups. She gasped 'Velvet, the library ...' and fainted. I went into the library and found Mrs Horsehair dead on the floor. She had been hit on the head. I looked around the room. The port decanter was lying smashed on the floor and there was broken glass everywhere. The ashtray was full of cigarette stubs – the kind that Mr Jeffrey smokes. I also noticed immediately that one of the large silver candlesticks was missing. Both the library window and the connecting door to the billiard room were open. I called for help, and Miss Daphne and young Mr Archibald came running in from the conservatory. Dame Christie and Myrtle Berry were next on the scene, followed by old Mr Archibald. Mr Oscarsson came in via the billiard room, followed a few seconds later by his actress friend, and last of all Mr Jeffrey came rushing in, calling for help, and shouting that he had found the vicar unconscious on the terrace.

Velvet

B What the maid heard

Around seven o'clock I went upstairs to put on my new uniform. Reverend Truelove, old Mr Archibald and his son, and a famous lady novelist were joining the weekend guests for dinner, so it was a formal occasion. As I got to the top of the stairs I heard angry voices coming from Mrs Horsehair's room, and guessed that Mrs Horsehair and her niece were having one of their rows. I tried not to listen, but couldn't help catching one phrase very distinctly. Mrs Horsehair shouted, 'If you marry him, you stupid little fool, I'll cast you off without a penny.' Then the door burst open, and Miss Daphne rushed out, sobbing. She ran straight to her own room and slammed the door.

I cam downstairs again about fifteen minutes later, and heard Mr Jeffery talking on the telephone in the hall. I tried not to listen, but I couldn't help overhearing one or two phrases: 'Can't you wait a bit longer – the old woman's so damned mean with her money ...'. There was a long pause then he said, 'I'll find the money somehow ...' and slammed the receiver down. I guessed he was talking to one of his gambling companions. Mr Jeffery is very fond of roulette, but his mother disapproves, and tries to prevent him gambling by keeping him short of money.

From a quarter past seven till eight o'clock I was in the kitchen preparing the food, but I peeped out to watch the guests arrive – young Mr Archibald looked very dashing in a blue velvet suit.

Dinner was at eight, and as soon as I came in with the soup, I noticed that things weren't going too well. Dame Christie and Myrtle Berry seemed to be getting on quite well discussing some murder in great detail, but Mr Jeffery looked like thunder, and young Mr Archibald looked terribly unhappy: he's passionately in love with Miss Daphne, you know. Daphne looked as if she were about to cry, and the actress, Miss Topless, looked a bit annoyed as well. This might have been because she and Miss Daphne were wearing exactly the same dress, or it might have been because her companion, Mr Oscarsson, and Mrs Horsehair were having a very intimate conversation at one end of the table. Reverend Truelove and old Mr Archibald tried to keep the conversation going, but it was quite a relief when dinner broke up at about nine o'clock. The ladies then retired to the parlour for coffee, and the gentlemen went to the billiard room. I served coffee, and then went back to the kitchen to clear up.

At about 9.45 I went into the parlour to collect the coffee cups, and as I crossed the hall, I overheard loud voices in the ballroom. I tried not to listen but it sounded very like Miss Topless. Suddenly the door opened, and Mrs Horsehair came out. She looked rather embarrassed on seeing me, and said, 'Oh, Charlotte, I was looking for my book. Do you know where it might be?' I said that I hadn't seen it, and she muttered something about looking in the library and made off in that direction.

I went on into the parlour where I found Dame Christie, Myrtle Berry, and old Mr Archibald deep in conversation. They were still talking about murder. I couldn't help listening. It made me feel quite cold, so I collected up the cups as slowly as I could. As I was doing this, I heard a door slam in the hall, followed by the sound of footsteps crossing the hall. Then the front door slammed. I finished collecting the cups, and went out into the hall, but no one was there. I started to cross the hall towards the kitchen, suddenly, I heard a piercing scream. It came from the library. I couldn't move. I tried to call for help, but couldn't make a sound. The kitchen door opened, and Velvet, the butler, came running out. He looked at me in astonishment. I gasped, 'The library ...' and then I fainted.

Charlotte

I arrived at Conkers for Sunday tea as usual, and was invited to return for dinner after Evensong. Before I left, Mrs Horsehair asked me to advise her on a certain problem, and we went into the library to discuss it. Mrs Horsehair then confided in me that she and the young film director Oscar Oscarsson, who was one of her weekend guests, were planning to marry. I expressed my approval of the project, congratulated her, and then enquired what the problem might be. She was worried, it appeared, about how the marriage might affect her son Jeffery. She thought he might disapprove of her remarrying so soon, and, furthermore, might object to her altering her will in favour of her new husband. I advised her to put her own interests first. She appeared satisfied with this, and I left the house.

I returned at about half past seven, after Evensong, and was shown into the parlour by Velvet, the butler. I was immediately conscious of a rather strained atmosphere, particularly among the young people. Daphne and Archibald looked very unhappy – although I put this down to a lovers' tiff – and Jeffery's face looked like a thundercloud. I wondered if his mother had broached the subject of her marriage. The older members of the party, however, a lady novelist and an American friend of Mrs Horsehair's seemed pleasant enough, although there was also an actress who I found distinctly unpleasant. However, I endeavoured to put them all at ease with one or two of my anecdotes in the usual style, and dinner passed quite pleasantly.

After dinner, we gentlemen retired to the billiard room for port and a game of snooker. The first game ended just before 9.30 and both Oscar and young Archibald excused themselves, saying they had urgent matters to attend to. The rest of us stood around talking until Velvet reappeared with the port. At that point our little party dispersed: Jeffery went to the library to finish off a letter, while old Archibald and I went to join the ladies in the parlour. I found the subject of conversation there rather distasteful, so after about ten minutes, I went for a quiet stroll and a smoke in the grounds. I had been there for about a quarter of an hour, enjoying the evening air and mentally composing next Sunday's sermon, when Jeffery came out of the house, slamming the front door behind him. He had taken off his formal dinner jacket, and was wearing a dark blue smoking jacket. I invited him to join me, but he only grunted and strode off into the shrubbery. I finished my pipe, and, hearing the church clock chime ten, I decided to go back into the house, to take my leave. As I was crossing the terrace, I became aware that someone was behind me. I started to turn, and, out of the corner of my eye, caught a flash of something blue, but, before I could make out who it was, a hand was pressed over my mouth and I felt someone strike me with a heavy object from behind. Everything went black, and I fell to the ground.

Reverend Truelove

1 Who was where?

Write the correct names of the rooms on the plan of the house. Mark where the characters were at 10 p.m. and where the body was found.

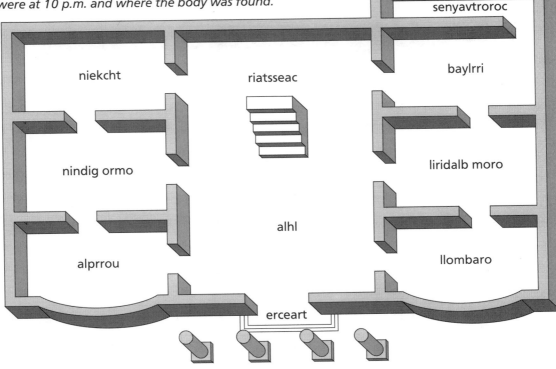

niekcht

riatsseac

senyavtroroc

baylrri

nindig ormo

liridalb moro

alhl

alprrou

llombaro

erceart

2 Who's who?

Draw a line to connect the name of the character with the description.

Charlotte

Velvet

Reverend Truelove

Mildred Horsehair

Daphne

Jeffery

Oscar Oscarsson

young Archibald

old Archibald

Myrtle Berry

Agatha Christie

Alice B Topless

an actress

the maid

the niece

the son

an influential, but
   impoverished film
   director

a dashing but penniless
   young man

an American lady

the butler

a rich widow in her 40s –
   the owner of the house

a neighbour

the local vicar

a lady novelist

3 The motives

Who might have had a motive for the crime and why?

4 The clues

Write a list of any clues that might help to find the murderer.

The murderer was:

Motive:

Maybe some people can read minds. Perhaps there is a prehistoric beast at the bottom of Loch Ness. Spiritualists could be in touch with those who have died, passing on their messages to us at a fiver a time.

But there is an alternative, rational, non-magical explanation available for all these mysteries. You might not accept it. You might think that it is more likely that people bend cutlery through the power of thought than by adept sleight of hand. But as William of Ockham pointed out, it is usually better to accept the explanation which doesn't require you to invent something new and unknown. For instance, corn circles might be created by little green men, or else by hoaxers. Take your pick – except that we know all about hoaxers; the world is full of them. Little green men have yet to put in an appearance.

People who do believe in the paranormal often appeal to the sceptics' sense of fair play. They imply that we sceptics are greedy when we say that there is a rational explanation for all the phenomena they come up with. Can't we be open minded, they ask, and allow them at least one or two miracles? Sorry, no. If you met someone who claimed that rain was the angels crying, you'd probably feel obliged to tell him that it was water vapour condensing in the atmosphere. And if he tried to claim that at least sometimes it was the angels crying, you'd have to be firm and say that it was absolutely always and invariably condensing water vapour.

Of course people hunger for the strange and wonderful. And they can find it. The dead walk and talk in my living room when I watch a video of *Casablanca*. I can sense what people thousands of miles away are thinking by calling them on the phone. And scientists are learning the secrets of the universe, from the tiniest particles of life in our bodies, to the origin of the most distant galaxies.

But these wonders are never enough for the paranormal brigade. They want more. Flying telephones. Ghostly tambourines. Bent spoons. Children who can detect a picture of a ship inside a lined, sealed envelope. Often they manage to persuade others that these are the result of weird, inexplicable happenings. People who are normally quite sensible, will say: 'Well, I don't understand – there must be something in it.'

Generally there isn't. But it's hard to find explanations. The press, particularly the tabloids, are in the business of creating wonderful mysteries, not explaining them. (Often the most absurd claims are printed without elaboration. For instance, in December 1989, Uri Geller claimed to have stopped Big Ben. The fact that he made this claim only after the clock had broken down did not, apparently, strike anyone as absurd.)

Does it all matter? After all, there's no harm in reading your horoscope in the daily paper. On the other hand, some people pay large sums to people who claim that their lives are being dominated by heavenly bodies millions of miles away. The wife of the heir to the throne consults astrologers. For several years the President of the US had his timetable drawn up in consultation with the planets.

Psychic healers, fire-walking teachers and others relieve people of large sums by offering them the false hope of a better life. Authors of innumerable 'occult' books make small fortunes by peddling nonsense to the gullible and the naïve. Even clever people are taken in if the rational, practical alternatives are not presented. Here are a few ...

A

BERMUDA TRIANGLE

This myth has been kicking round for more than a hundred years, but really came to public attention with Charles Berlitz's 1974 book *The Bermuda Triangle Mystery*. Allegedly within this area of sea vast numbers of ships and planes have disappeared completely, mysteriously and without trace. It's sometimes claimed that they have been 'stolen' by flying saucers, and that the crews are still alive on some other plane, this time an astral one. This is a classic example of creating a mystery where none exists. Nearly all the accidents had normal causes, such as bad weather, almost always ignored by Triangle writers. Stories are copied from book to book and article to article, often embellished with fresh, inaccurate details at each stage. In his book, *The Bermuda Triangle Mystery – Solved*, Larry Kusche examines many of the disasters and finds all of them explicable.

For example, the all-time favourite Triangle mystery involves Flight 19; five US Army Air Corps planes which were lost together in 1945. All manned by experienced aircrew, they are supposed to have disappeared for no reason, out of a clear sky, while in no apparent peril.

In fact Flight 19 was a training flight, led by a lieutenant who was unfamiliar with the area and whose two compasses had malfunctioned. The weather was poor. Radio messages indicated that the flight – lacking modern guidance systems – had become hopelessly lost soon after take-off. They had only enough fuel to fly until 7 pm, shortly after the last radio messages were received.

In other words, no mystery at all. But as in the other Triangle cases, the promulgators leave out any information which doesn't suit their case.

B

CORN CIRCLES

On the night of Saturday 11 July this year, in a field in Buckinghamshire, 12 teams set about creating corn circles and geometric patterns without the use of artificial light. The magnificent results were visible by daylight, and one team won the £3,000 prize – proof if it were needed that there is no problem about making corn patterns, as hoaxers have already admitted.

This of course has not prevented the battier 'cereologists' from declaring that the fact that some people fake some corn circles does not mean that others aren't being made by visitors from outer space. As John Martineau of the Centre for Crop Circle Studies said afterwards, 'You could say that corn circles are the entrance to fairyland ... I think we are being told of other lands.' But there is no evidence that crop circle experts can tell the difference between circles made by self-confessed hoaxers and those so far 'unexplained'.

By the same token, we know that many toys are made by people in factories. This does not, of course, prove that the rest aren't made by elves in Santa's workshop.

There has been much anguishing over the fact that corn circles are more common in Britain than in any other country. This could indicate that there is more psychic energy here, or that space aliens are particularly interested in us. Or it could show that there has been an awful lot of publicity here.

CRYPTOZOOLOGY

This is the study of mysterious and probably non-existent creatures, of whom much the best known is our own Loch Ness monster. Sadly, there is scarcely a scintilla of evidence for Nessie. Tales of sightings before the twentieth century are either untraceable or else refer to beasts in different bodies of water. The original picture which started the craze, the 'Surgeon's photo' of 1933, is easy to duplicate with a cut-out model and was taken suspiciously close to April Fool's Day that year.

Other sightings turn out to be mistakes or hoaxes. Otters playing in the water could easily look like a moving serpent. Deer sometimes swim across the loch. Flat water, especially in poor light or with atmospheric refraction, can play tricks on the eyes, making schools of fish or even floating logs look like a monster.

In 1972 the Robert Rines expedition produced a remarkable photo of what looks like a flipper taken in the loch. Based on this, Sir Peter Scott went on to paint a picture of the whole monster, looking like a pleiosaur, a prehistoric water animal. Yet this picture was extrapolated from a retouched version of a computer-enhanced print of a negative which showed almost nothing at all.

In his fascinating book, *Pseudoscience and the Paranormal*, Terence Hines asks how it is that several examples of the five-foot long coelacanth, which was thought to have become extinct 200 million years ago, have been discovered in the vastness of the Indian Ocean, while we appear incapable of finding a far bigger beast in a 25-mile lake.

Much the same combination of hoaxes and mistakes probably accounts for the Himalayan Yeti and for Bigfoot, the shambling half-man, half-beast alleged to live in the north-western US. In both cases the sightings are probably of bears, seen in the distance on their hind legs. In similar fashion, the shy orangutan was once thought to be the mysterious Wild Man of Borneo.

UFOs

Of course UFOs exist. The term stands for Unidentified Flying Object, and there are plenty of those littering the skies. The question is whether they are alien visitors from outer space, or aircraft, weather balloons, the Northern Lights, or nearby street lamps refracted in the haze. Evidence for flying saucers is regrettably short and what there is of it is highly suspect. The first person to spot a 'flying saucer' was a civilian pilot named Kenneth Arnold in 1947. He reported seeing nine moving objects flying 'like a saucer would if you skipped it across water'. Four years later one George Adamski announced that he had met a Venusian in the Californian desert.

Unfortunately there is no chance that any of these accounts is true. The late Christopher Evans, an experimental psychologist, wearily explained why in his 1974 book *Cults of Unreason*.

Although there may be advanced civilisations in space, most of the solar systems in our part of the galaxy are at least 200 light years distant. Assuming that these civilisations had invented travel at close to the speed of light, it would still take them more than two centuries to get here. Evans reckoned this might make their visits rather infrequent – 'perhaps every 10,000 or 50,000 years'.

Rather than guess at how Vulkans could have managed to conquer the laws of physics, time would be better spent investigating the witnesses of their arrival. Although George Adamski bills himself in his book as 'a philosopher, student, teacher and saucer researcher', he in fact worked a hamburger stall on the road to the Mount Palomar observatory. Kenneth Arnold later claimed (against statistical odds) to have seen UFOs on seven subsequent occasions. Invisible entities, what is more, once paid him a visit. 'I was aware of their presence,' he stated, 'because I could see my rugs and furniture sink down under their weight.'

COLD READING

This is the technique used by innumerable charlatans, including fortune tellers, palmists, astrologers and spiritualists – anyone who wants to appear to have a unique, paranormal method of finding out about complete strangers. It is not too difficult to learn, but it does require hard work, cunning and acute observation, plus a certain amount of sheer fraud. Luckily there are plenty of how-to-do-it books available. The techniques are many, but they all rely on the suspension of scepticism by the customer who, after all, has paid the money in the hope of receiving reassurance, or to get a message from a departed loved one, and who is anxious for the cold reader to succeed.

One standard technique is to use general statements which people think refer uniquely to them, but which could apply to almost all of us. 'You are sometimes too sensitive ... you occasionally let your good nature get the better of you ... now and again you are aggressive and regret it later ...' The customer's reply often provides further information which can be parlayed into more surprising knowledge.

The late Mrs Doris Stokes, the 'spirit medium' who did both individual sessions and mass gatherings in concert halls, was a remarkably skilled cold reader. She would produce a stream of guesses, a few of which were inevitably correct. Mistakes were either ignored, or turned to her advantage. (Announcing that a man had died from a heart attack, she was told he had in fact been thrown from a motorbike. Without missing a beat she said, 'Yes, dear, but he had the heart attack just before he came off,' thus turning a rotten guess into a fake 'hit'.) Her warm, cosy manner made it seem impossible that such a delightful old lady could be a fraud.

Sometimes distressed people phoned her home, and were encouraged to tell their story by her husband, who then offered free tickets to her next show. When the people appeared she seemed to have a miraculous knowledge of their circumstances. Either they had forgotten the chat with Mr Stokes, or else were too polite to say: 'I told you that'. Other listeners were mightily impressed. Mistakes were blamed on the fact that many dead people were trying to talk to her at once, and that their 'lines' were crossed.

The trick largely depended on the great goodwill of her customers. Years ago, after we had scorned a reading in which she had not even realised that the child she was talking about was dead, we got an angry letter from the boy's mother. She was cross, not with Mrs Stokes for being so spectacularly wrong, but with us, for spoiling what to her had been a powerful emotional occasion.

PSYCHIC DETECTIVES

The detailed forensic approach to detection, although it was good enough for Sherlock Holmes, does not always produce quick results. And as soon as a high-profile police investigation looks as if it has got bogged down, the chances are you will read that a helpful psychic is offering his or her assistance.

Sometimes mediums do appear to strike lucky. Most famously, the psychic Nella Jones credits herself with having been ahead of the police in their pursuit of the Yorkshire Ripper. In her autobiography *Ghost of a Chance*, published in 1982, Jones wrote: 'Eighteen months before police arrested the man they said was the Yorkshire Ripper, I had drawn the killer's face, described where he lived and worked, and predicted two more murders before he was caught.'

The drawing (made 14 months before Peter Sutcliffe was caught) in fact bore no resemblance to him. As for describing where he lived, Jones had said: 'Stop him at the city centre. Go to Chapel Street ... the number six flashed across my mind, the name Joyce ... a wrought iron gate in front ... a small garage nearby but I didn't know if it belonged to the house or was a separate business.'

Sutcliffe lived at 6 Garden Lane, Heaton, Bradford. So although Jones was right about the number, she was wrong about the city centre, wrong about the name Joyce and at best half-right about the 'small garage'.

In November 1980 Jones claimed that Sutcliffe was about to claim another victim, possibly within a week. Mercifully, there were no more victims. Recently Jones told a researcher working for the psychic investigator James Randi that she was about to be declared an official police psychic and that New Scotland Yard had validated her claims.

Randi says: 'We were told by Inspector Edward Ellison of the Yard that they never approach psychics for information; there are no official police psychics; they do not endorse psychics in any way; and there is no recorded instance of any psychic solving a criminal case or providing evidence or information that led directly to its solution.'

TELEPATHY

A Gallop poll last year found that a third of Americans believe in telepathy – communication, that is, between two people without using any of the five senses. Twenty-five per cent of Americans claim to have actually had a telepathic experience. 'Telepathy,' says Carl Shrager, editor of *American Psychic* magazine, 'is really our sixth sense, the shadow sense that people accept to varying degrees. Knowing who's on the phone when it rings is probably the most common everyday telepathic experience.'

Yet correctly guessing from time to time who is on the phone before you answer it should hardly be a matter of great surprise. Given the limited number of people who call any one of us in a year, and given our knowledge of how long it is since someone last called and of the possible reasons for their calling, you and I could make an educated guess as to who will ring us next. 'I thought it was going to be you,' we shall say smugly if we are right, but we will keep quiet and quickly forget if it turns out to be someone else. Only if we were right almost all the time should we begin to wonder – but then no one ever is.

This lack of consistency is not confined to amateurs. Professional mind-readers consistently fail to repeat under scientific conditions what initially appear to have been extraordinary results. Studies with the most consistent success rates are invariably those done under the least stringent conditions and employing the weakest methodology.

To date, not a single repeatable scientifically controlled experiment in which subjects have been asked to guess unseen numbers, pictures, shapes or playing cards has shown results higher than would be predicted by the laws of probability. The problem is that most people are bad at estimating probabilities, usually wildly overestimating the chances against something happening.

Unscientific tests produce much more exciting results. The Amazing Kreskin, a leading mentalist, used to ask audiences to think of an odd two-digit number less than 50 with the restriction that the two digits cannot be the same. Kreskin would announce he has received the number 37, although he was initially going to say 35. Hands would shoot up all over the theatre – impressive until you read the survey that found that on average 56 per cent of people will pick either 35 or 37 when given these instructions.

BIORHYTHMS

This theory suggests that our lives are dominated by three fixed cycles which begin on the day of our birth. The physical cycle lasts 23 days, the emotional 28 and the intellectual 33. You can even buy a pocket calculator, key in your birth date, and work out where you are placed for all three cycles every day.

For each cycle, it's alleged, you will be comfortable and successful in that aspect of your life on high days; the reverse on low days. The very best days are when all three are high, though since the number in each cycle have no common factors, you will reach an absolute peak for all three together only once every 21,252 days, or 58 years. Equally, they will all meet at the bottom only once in most people's lives.

Biorhythm 'science' was allegedly invented and tested by three European researchers earlier this century. Sadly, almost none of their work survives, though one, a Hermann Swoboda of Vienna, claimed that 'eight trunks' of his research documents were stolen by Russian troops in 1945. This has not prevented the missing 'findings' from being much quoted in biorhythm books and articles.

Proponents often cash in on the fact that humans are indeed subject to certain rhythms, such as the circadian rhythm, which helps cause jet lag, and the menstrual cycle. These acknowledged phenomena are cited as support for the pseudo-science of biorhythms. Advocates also like to 'prove' their case by citing specific examples. Marilyn Monroe killed herself on bad days for both her emotional and intellectual cycles.

One favourite story concerns Arnold Palmer, who won the 1962 British Open when high in all three cycles. A fortnight later he lot the PGA when he was low in all three. So William Bainbridge of the University of Washington analysed all the tournaments Palmer won from 1955 to 1971. He found that he won considerably less often when his physical cycle was alleged to be high. A 1979 Transport and Road Research Laboratory report which examined the biorhythms of 112,560 drivers involved in accidents concluded that 'convincing evidence was not found to support the biorhythm theory'.

Complete the information in the boxes.

	(i) What it is	(ii) Evidence for	(iii) Evidence against
A Bermuda Triangle			
B Corn Circles			
C Cryptozoology			
D UFOs			
E Cold Reading			
F Psychic Detectives			
G Telepathy			
H Biorhythms			

THE FROG PRINCE

In olden times, when people could have all they wished for at once, lived a king who had many beautiful daughters; but the youngest was so lovely, that the sun himself would wonder whenever he shone on her face. Near to the king's castle lay a dark, gloomy forest, in the midst of which stood an old linden tree, shading with its foliage the pleasant waters of a fountain.

One day, when the weather was very hot, the king's daughter came into the forest, and seated herself on the side of the cool fountain, and when at last the silence became wearisome, she began to toss a golden ball in the air, and catch it again, as an amusement. Presently, however, the king's daughter failed to catch the golden ball in her hand, so that it fell on the ground, and rolled over the grass into the water.

The princess followed it with her eyes till it disappeared, for the water was so deep that she could not see the bottom.

Then she cried aloud, and began to weep bitterly for the loss of her golden ball. Presently she heard a voice exclaiming:

'Why do you weep, O king's daughter? Your tears could melt even the stones to pity you!' ✂ (5)

She looked at the spot from whence the voice came, and saw a frog stretching his thick ugly head out of the water.

'Oh! there you are, old water-paddler,' she said. 'Well, then, I am crying for the loss of my golden ball that has fallen into the fountain.'

'Then weep no more,' answered the frog; 'I can get it for you. But what will you give me if I fetch your plaything?'

'Oh! anything you like, dear frog,' she replied. 'What will you have – my dresses, my pearls and jewels, or the golden crown I wear sometimes?'

'Neither,' answered the frog. 'Your clothes, your pearls and your jewels, or even your golden crown, are nothing to me. I want you to love me, and let me be your companion and playfellow. I should like to sit at your table, eat from your golden plate, and drink out of your cup, and sleep in your nice little bed. If you will promise me all this, then I will dive down into the water and bring up your pretty golden ball.'

'Oh yes!' she replied. 'I will promise you anything you like if you will only bring up my ball again.'

But she thought to herself that a silly, chattering frog as he was, living in the water with others like himself, and croaking, could not be fit to associate with mankind. ✂ (4)

The frog, who believed in the promise of the king's daughter, dipped his head under the water, and sank down to the bottom, where he quickly found the ball, and seizing it in his mouth, carried it to the surface and threw it on the grass. When the king's daughter saw the beautiful plaything, she was full of joy, and, catching it up, ran away as fast as she could run. ✂ (5)

'Wait, wait,' cried the frog, 'take me with you, I cannot run so fast as you can.' But the young princess would not listen to the frog's croaking; she got to the house as fast as she could, and soon forgot the poor frog, who was obliged to return to the fountain, and remain there. ✂ (3)

The next day, however, while the princess was sitting with the king and his courtiers, and eating out of her own little golden plate, she heard a strange noise on the marble steps outside, splish, splash, splish, splash, and presently came a knock at the door, and a voice cried, 'Lovely princess, open the door for me.' So she rose and went to see who could be outside; but when she caught sight of the frog, she closed the door hastily and seated herself again at the table, looking quite pale. The king, seeing that his daughter was alarmed, said to her, 'My child, what is there at the door? Is it a giant come to carry you away?'

'Oh no, my father!' she replied; 'it is no giant, only a great ugly frog.'

'A frog! What can he want with you, my daughter?'

'Ah, my dear father, I will tell you all about it. Yesterday, when I was playing with my golden ball by the fountain in the forest, I let it fall into the water, and because I cried, the frog fetched it out for me, and he made me promise that he should come to the castle and be my companion, for I thought he could not get out of the water to come to me, and now here he is.'

Just then came a second knock at the door, and a voice cried:

'King's daughter, king's daughter, open for me;

You promised that I your companion should be.

When you sat in the shade from the sun's bright beam.

And I fetched up your ball from the fountain's cool stream.' ✄ (4 + 5)

'Then,' said the king, 'my daughter, you must keep your promise; go and let him in at once.' So she was obliged to go and open the door, and the frog hopped in after her close to her feet and quite up to her chair. But when she sat down he cried: 'Take me up by you.' She would not at first, till her father obliged her to lift the frog on the chair by her side. He was no sooner there than he jumped upon the table and said: 'Now, then, push your little golden plate nearer, and we will eat together.' The princess did as he told her, but everyone could see how much she disliked it. The frog seemed to relish his dinner very much, but he would give the princess half of all he took. At last he said: 'I have eaten and drank quite enough, and I feel very tired, so now carry me upstairs into your little bedroom, and make your silken bed ready, that we may sleep together.'

When the princess heard this, she began to weep, for she was really afraid of the cold frog: she could not even touch him, and now he actually wanted to sleep in her neat beautiful little bed.

But the king was displeased at her tears, and he said: 'He who helped you when you were in trouble must not be despised now.' So the young princess found she must obey. Then she took up the frog with two fingers, and holding him as far from her as possible, she carried him upstairs and placed him in a corner of her room. ✄ (3)

In the evening, however, as soon as the princess was in bed, the frog crept out of his corner and said to her: 'I am so tired; lift me up, and let me sleep in your bed, or I will tell your father.' ✄ (4)

On hearing this, the princess fell into a great passion, so seizing the frog in her hand, she dashed him with all her strength against the wall, saying: 'You will be quiet now, I hope, you ugly frog.'

But as he fell, how surprised she was to see the frog change into a handsome young prince, with beautiful friendly eyes, who afterwards became her constant companion, and at last her father gave his consent to their marriage. ✄ (5)

Before it took place, however, the prince told them his history, how he had been changed into a frog by a wicked witch, and that she had condemned him to live in the fountains until a king's daughter should come and release him. No one else in the world had the power to do so.

After they married, the young prince proposed that he should take his bride to his own kingdom. So on the wedding day a splendid carriage drawn by eight white horses drove up to the door. They had white feathers on their heads and golden harness, and by the side of the carriage stood the prince's steward, the faithful Harry. This faithful Harry had been so unhappy when his master was changed into a frog, that he had fastened three iron bands round his heart, to prevent it from bursting with woe and sorrow.

The carriage with the prince and his bride soon drove away with Harry behind in his old place, and full of joy at the release of his master. They had not travelled far when they heard a loud crack – as if something had broken.

Now, the prince knew nothing of the iron bands round his servant's heart, so he cried out: 'Harry, is the carriage breaking?'

'No, sire,' he replied, 'only the iron bands which I bound round my heart for fear it should burst with sorrow while you were a frog confined to the fountain. They are breaking now because I am so happy to see my master restored to his own shape, and travelling to his kingdom with a beautiful bride.'

The prince and princess never forgot faithful Harry, who had loved his master so well while he was in trouble.

THE FROG MAIDEN

An old couple was childless, and the husband and the wife longed for a child. So when the wife found that she was with child, they were over-joyed; but to their great disappointment, the wife gave birth not to a human child, but to a little she-frog. However, as the little frog spoke and behaved as a human child, not only the parents but also the neighbours came to love her and called her affectionately 'Little Miss Frog'.

Some years later the woman died, and the man decided to marry again. The woman he chose was a widow with two ugly daughters and they were very jealous of Little Miss Frog's popularity with the neighbours. All three took a delight in ill-treating Little Miss Frog.

One day the youngest of the king's four sons announced that he would perform the hair-washing ceremony on a certain date and he invited all young ladies to join in the ceremony, as he would choose at the end of the ceremony one of them to be his princess.

On the morning of the appointed day the two ugly sisters dressed themselves in fine raiment, and with great hopes of being chosen by the prince they started for the palace. Little Miss Frog ran after them, and pleaded, 'Sisters, please let me come with you.' ✂ **(5)**

The sisters laughed and said mockingly, 'What, the little frog wants to come? The invitation is to young ladies and not to young frogs.' Little Miss Frog walked along with them towards the palace, pleading for permission to come. But the sisters were adamant, and so at the palace gates she was left behind. However, she spoke so sweetly to the guards that they allowed her to go in. Little Miss Frog found hundreds of young ladies gathered round the pool full of lilies in the palace grounds; and she took her place among them and waited for the prince. ✂ **(4)**

The prince now appeared, and washed his hair in the pool. The ladies also let down their hair and joined in the ceremony. At the end of the ceremony, the prince declared that as the ladies were all beautiful, he did not know whom to choose and so he would throw a posy of jasmines into the air; and the lady on whose head the posy fell would be his princess. The prince then threw the posy into the air, and all the ladies present looked up expectantly. The posy, however, fell on Little Miss Frog's head, to the great annoyance of the ladies, especially the two stepsisters. The prince also was disappointed, but he felt that he should keep his word. So Little Miss Frog was married to the prince, and she became Little Princess Frog. ✂ **(3)**

Some time later, the old king called his four sons to him and said, 'My sons, I am now too old to rule the country, and I want to retire to the forest and become a hermit. So I must appoint one of you as my successor. As I love you all alike, I will give you a task to perform, and he who performs it successfully shall be king in my palace. The task is, bring me a golden deer at sunrise on the seventh day from now.' ✂ **(5)**

The youngest prince went home to Little Princess Frog and told her about the task. 'What, only a golden deer!' exclaimed Princess Frog. 'Eat as usual, my prince, and on the appointed day I will give you a golden deer.'

So the youngest prince stayed at home, while the three elder princes went into the forest in search of the deer.

On the seventh day before sunrise, Little Princess Frog woke up her husband and said, 'Go to the palace, prince, and here is your golden deer.'

The young prince looked, then rubbed his eyes, and looked again. There was no mistake about it; the deer which Little Princess Frog was holding by a lead was really of pure gold. So he went to the palace, and to the great annoyance of the elder princes who brought ordinary deers, he was declared to be the heir by the king. The elder princes, however, pleaded for a second chance, and the king reluctantly agreed.

'Then perform this second task,' said the king. 'On the seventh day from now at sunrise, you must bring me the rice that never becomes stale, and the meat that is ever fresh. ✂ **(4)**

Reading Games, © Jill Hadfield and Charles Hadfield 1995

The youngest prince went home and told Princess Frog about the new task. 'Don't you worry, sweet prince,' said Princess Frog. 'Eat as usual, sleep as usual, and on the appointed day I will give you the rice and meat.'

So the youngest prince stayed at home, while the three elder princes went in search of the rice and meat.

On the seventh day at sunrise, Little Princess Frog woke up her husband and said, 'My Lord, go to the palace now, and here is your rice and meat.'

The youngest prince took the rice and meat, and went to the palace, and to the great annoyance of the elder princes who brought only well-cooked rice and meat, he was again declared to be the heir. ✂ (3 + 5)

But the two elder princes again pleaded for one more chance, and the king said, 'This is positively the last task. On the seventh day from now at sunrise, bring me the most beautiful woman on this earth.'

'Ho, ho!' said the three elder princes to themselves in great joy. 'Our wives are very beautiful, and we will bring them. One of us is sure to be declared heir, and our good-for-nothing brother will be nowhere this time.'

The youngest prince overheard their remark, and felt sad, for his wife was a frog and ugly. When he reached home, he said to his wife, 'Dear Princess, I must go and look for the most beautiful woman on this earth. My brothers will bring their wives, for they are really beautiful, but I will find someone who is more beautiful.'

'Don't you fret, my prince,' replied Princess Frog. 'Eat as usual, sleep as usual, and you can take me to the palace on the appointed day; surely I shall be declared to be the most beautiful woman.'

The youngest prince looked at the princess in surprise; but he did not want to hurt her feelings, and he said gently, 'All right Princess, I will take you with me on the appointed day.' ✂ (4)

On the seventh day at dawn, Little Princess Frog woke up the prince and said, 'My Lord, I must make myself beautiful. So please wait outside and call me when it is nearly time to go.' The prince left the room as requested. After some moments, the prince shouted from outside, 'Princess, it is time for us to go.' ✂ (5)

'Please wait, my Lord,' replied the princess, 'I am just powdering my face.'

After some moments the prince shouted, 'Princess, we must go now.'

'All right, my Lord,' replied the princess, 'please open the door for me.'

The prince thought to himself, 'Perhaps, just as she was able to obtain the golden deer and the wonderful rice and meat, she is able to make herself beautiful, and he expectantly opened the door, but he was disappointed to see Little Princess Frog still a frog and as ugly as ever. However, so as not to hurt her feelings, the prince said nothing and took her along to the palace. When the prince entered the audience chamber with his Frog Princess the three elder princes with their wives were already there. The king looked at the prince in surprise and said, 'Where is your beautiful maiden?'

'I will answer for the prince, my king,' said the Frog Princess. 'I am his beautiful maiden.' She then took off her frog skin and stood a beautiful maiden dressed in silk and satin. The king declared her to be the most beautiful maiden in the world, and selected the prince as his successor on the throne.

The prince asked his princess never to put on the ugly frog skin again, and the Frog Princess, to accede to his request, threw the skin into the fire.

CINDERELLA

Once upon a time the wife of a rich man fell sick, and as she knew her end was approaching, she called her only daughter to her bedside, and said, 'Dear child, when I am gone continue good and pious, and Heaven will help you in every trouble, and I will be your guardian angel.'

Soon after this the mother closed her eyes in death, and day after day the maiden went to her mother's grave to weep. But she never forgot her last words, and continued pious and gentle to all around her. Winter came and covered the grave with its dazzling drapery of snow; but when the bright sun of spring again warmed the earth, the husband had taken to himself another wife. This wife had been already married, and she brought with her two daughters who were fair and beautiful in appearance, while at heart they were evil-minded and malicious. It soon became a very sad time for their poor stepsister, of whom they were very envious, and at last persuaded their mother to send her to the kitchen.

'Is the stupid goose to sit in the parlour with us?' they said. 'Those who eat ought to work. Send her into the kitchen with the kitchen-maid.'

Then they took away all her nice clothes, and gave her an ugly old frock and wooden shoes, which she was obliged to put on.

'Look at our fine princess now! See how she has dressed herself!' they said, laughing, and driving her into the kitchen.

And there she was obliged to remain doing hard work from morning till night; and she had to rise early to draw water, to light the fire, to cook, and to wash. Besides all this, her stepsisters invented all sorts of ways to make her more unhappy. They would either treat her with scorn or else push her out of their way so roughly that she sometimes fell among the pea shells and cabbage leaves that lay in the yard. ✂ (5)

At night, when she was tired with her work, she had no bed to lie on, and when the weather was cold she would creep into the ashes on the warm hearth, and get so black and smutty that they gave her the name of Cinderella. ✂ (4)

It happened one day that the father was going to a fair, and he asked his two stepdaughters what he should bring back for them as a present.

'A beautiful dress,' said the eldest; 'a pearl necklace,' said her sister.

'And, Cinderella,' asked her father, 'what will you have?'

'Father,' she replied, 'please bring me the first twig that strikes your hat on your way home.'

So the father bought for his stepdaughters a beautiful dress and pearl necklace, and, as he was returning home, he rode through a shrubbery, where the green bushes clustered thickly around him, and a hazel twig stretching across his path struck his hat. Then he stopped, broke off the twig, and carried it home with him.

As soon as he reached the house he gave his stepdaughters the presents they had wished for, and to Cinderella the hazel twig from the hazel bush. She thanked him for it even more than her sisters had done for the beautiful presents, and went out immediately to her mother's grave, where she planted the hazel twig, and wept over it so much that her tears fell and softened the earth. ✂ (3)

The twig grew and became a beautiful tree, and Cinderella went three times every day to pray and weep at the grave; and on each visit a little white bird would perch on the tree, and when she expressed a wish, the bird would throw down whatever she wished for. ✂ (5)

After a time the king of the country gave a grand ball, which was to continue for three days. All the beautiful young ladies in the land were invited to this ball, so that the king's son might make a choice of a bride from amongst them.

The two stepsisters, when they heard that they were invited, knew not how to contain themselves for joy. They called Cinderella in haste, and said, 'Come and dress our hair and trim our shoes with gold buckles, for we are going to the ball at the king's palace.'

When Cinderella heard this she began to cry, for she was fond of dancing, and she wanted to go with her stepsisters, so she went to her stepmother and begged to be allowed to accompany them.

'You, Cinderella!' cried her stepmother, 'so covered with dirt and smut as you are; you go to a ball! Besides, you have no dress nor dancing shoes.'

Then she turned her back on the poor girl and hastened away with her two proud daughters to the ball. ✂ **(4)** There was no one at home now, so she went out to her mother's grave and stood under the hazel-tree and cried:

> 'Shake and shiver, little tree,
> With gold and silver cover me.'

Then the bird in the tree threw down a beautiful silk dress embroidered with gold and silver, and a new pair of glittering golden slippers. In great haste she dressed herself in these beautiful clothes and went to the ball. When she entered the ballroom, looking so beautiful in her rich dress and slippers, her stepmother and sisters did not know her; indeed, they took her for a foreign princess.

The king's son took a great deal of notice of this unknown lady, and danced with her several times, till at last he would dance with no other, always saying, 'This is my partner.' So she danced all the evening till it was time to go home, and the prince said he would accompany her, for he wanted to discover where she lived. But she avoided him, and with one bound she vanished. When the stepmother and her daughters reached home, they found her in her smutty dress, lying in the ashes, and a dingy little lamp burning on the chimney-piece. ✂ **(5)**

A short time after this the king gave another ball, to which her parents and stepsisters were invited. She again went to her mother's grave and said to the tree:

> 'Shake and rustle, little tree,
> Throw gold and silver over me.'

Then the bird threw down a most magnificent dress, more glittering and elegant than ever, and the brightest pair of gilded slippers. ✂ **(3)**

When she appeared at the fête in this dress, everyone was astonished at her beauty. The prince danced only with her, and to every other proposal replied, 'This is my partner'. When the time came to leave, she wanted to go, and the prince wished to accompany her, but she darted away from him and vanished so quickly that he could not follow her. ✂ **(4)**

Now, the king's son had had recourse to stratagem in the hope of discovering the home of the lovely princess. He had ordered the steps of the castle to be strewed with pitch, so that as she hurried away her left slipper stuck to the steps, and she was obliged to leave it behind. The prince himself picked it up; it was very small and elegant, and covered with gold.

The next morning he sent for one of his servants and said to him, 'None other shall be my bride but the lady to whom that slipper belongs, and whose foot it shall fit.' ✂ **(5)**

When the stepsisters heard of this proclamation from the prince they were delighted, for they both had small feet. The messenger went with the slipper from house to house, and the young ladies who had been present at the ball tried to put it on, but it would fit none of them, and at last he came to the two sisters. It would fit neither of them.

'Hast thou not another daughter?' asked the prince.
'None,' he said, 'excepting the child of my first wife; she could not possibly be your bride.'
'Send for her,' said the prince.
But the stepmother answered, 'Oh no! I dare not let you see her, she is much too dirty.'
But the prince insisted that she should be sent for, so at last they called her in.

After washing her hands and face, she made her appearance, and bowed to the prince, who offered her the golden shoe. She seated herself on a footstool, took off the heavy wooden shoe from her left foot, and slipped on the golden slipper, which fitted her exactly. Then, as she lifted up her head and looked at the king, he recognised the beautiful maiden who had danced with him at the ball, and exclaimed, 'That is the right bride!'

The stepmother and her two daughters were in a dreadful rage when they heard this.

But the prince disregarded their anger, and taking her on his horse, rode away with her. As they passed the hazel-tree on the grass, the two white doves cried:

> 'Fair maid and true,
> No blood in her shoe;
> She is the bride,
> With the prince by her side.'

BEAUTY AND POCK FACE

There were once two sisters; the eldest was very beautiful and everyone called her 'Beauty'; but the younger had a face covered with pock marks, and everyone called her 'Pock Face'. She was the daughter of the second wife, and was very spoilt, and had a bad character. Beauty's mother had died when her daughter was very small, and after her death she had turned into a yellow cow, which lived in the garden. Beauty adored the yellow cow, but it had a miserable existence, because the stepmother treated it so badly.

One day, the stepmother took the ugly daughter to the theatre and left the elder one at home. She wanted to accompany them, but her stepmother said: 'I will take you tomorrow, if you tidy the hemp in my room.'

Beauty went off and sat down in front of the stack of hemp, but after a long time she had only divided half. Bursting into tears, she took it off to the yellow cow, who swallowed the whole mass and then spat it out again all clearly arranged bit by bit. Beauty dried her tears, and gave the hemp to her mother on her return home: 'Mother, here is the hemp. I can go to the theatre tomorrow, can't I?'

But when the next day came, her stepmother again refused to take her, saying: 'You can go when you have separated the sesame seeds from the beans.' The poor girl had to divide them seed by seed, until the exhausting task made her eyes ache. Again she went to the yellow cow, who said to her: 'You stupid girl, you must separate them with a fan.' Now she understood, and the sesame and beans were soon divided. When she brought the seeds all nicely separated, her stepmother knew that she could no longer prevent her going to the theatre, but she asked her: 'How can a servant girl be so clever? Who helped you?' And Beauty had to admit that the yellow cow had advised her, which made the stepmother very angry. Without, therefore, saying a word, she killed and ate the cow, but Beauty had loved the cow so dearly that she could not eat its flesh. Instead, she put the bones in an earthenware pot and hid them in her bedroom. ✂ (5)

Day after day, the stepmother did not take her to the theatre, and one evening, when she had gone there herself with Pock Face, Beauty was so cross that she smashed everything in the house including the earthenware pot. Whereupon there was a crack, and a white horse, a new dress, and a pair of embroidered shoes came out. The sudden appearance of these things gave her a terrible fright, but she soon saw that they were real objects and, quickly pulling on the new dress and the shoes, she jumped on to the horse and rode out of the gate. ✂ (4)

While riding along, one of her shoes slipped off into the ditch. She wanted to dismount and fetch it, but could not do so; at the same time she did not want to leave it lying there. She was in a real quandary, when a fishmonger appeared. 'Brother fishmonger! Please pick up my shoe,' she said to him. He answered with a grin: 'With great pleasure, if you will marry me.' 'Who could marry you?' she said crossly. 'Fishmongers always stink.' And seeing that he had no chance, the fishmonger went on his way. Next, an assistant of a rice shop went by, and she said to him: 'Brother rice broker, please give me my shoe.' 'Certainly, if you will marry me,' said the young man. 'Marry a rice broker! Their bodies are all covered with dust.' The rice broker departed, and soon an oil merchant came by, whom she also asked to pick up her shoe. 'I will pick it up if you consent to marry me,' he replied. 'Who could want to marry you?' Beauty said with a sigh. 'Oil merchants are always so greasy.' Shortly after a scholar came by, whom she also asked to pick up her shoe. The scholar turned to look at her, and then said: 'I will do so at once if you promise to marry me.' The scholar was very handsome, so she nodded her head in agreement, and he picked up the shoe and put it on her foot. Then he took her back to his house and made her his wife. ✂ (3)

Three days later, Beauty went with her husband to pay the necessary respects to her parents. Her stepmother and sister had quite changed their manner and treated them both in the most friendly and attentive fashion. In the evening, they wanted to keep Beauty at home, and she, thinking they meant it kindly, agreed to stay and to follow her husband in a few days. ✂ (5)

The next morning her sister took her by the hand and said to her with a laugh: 'Sister, come and look into the well. We will see which of us is the more beautiful.' Suspecting nothing, Beauty went to the well and leant over to look down, but at this moment her sister gave her a shove and pushed her into the well, which she quickly covered up with a basket. Poor Beauty lost consciousness and was drowned.

After ten days, the scholar began to wonder why his wife had still not returned. He sent a messenger to inquire, and the stepmother sent back a message that his wife was suffering from a bad attack of smallpox and was not well enough to return for the moment. The scholar believed this, and every day he sent over salted eggs and other sickbed delicacies, all of which found their way into the stomach of the ugly sister. ✂ (4)

Reading Games, © Jill Hadfield and Charles Hadfield 1995

After two months, the stepmother was irritated by the continual messages from the scholar and made up her mind to practise a deception, and to send back her own daughter as his wife. The scholar was horrified when he saw her and said: 'Goodness! How changed you are! Surely you are not Beauty. My wife was never such a monster. Good Heavens!' Pock Face replied seriously: 'If I am not Beauty, whom do you think I am then? You know perfectly well I was very ill with smallpox and now you want to disown me. I shall die! I shall die!' And she began to howl. The tender-hearted scholar could not bear to see her weeping, and although he still had some doubts, he begged her forgiveness and tried to console her, so that gradually she stopped weeping.

Beauty, however, had been transformed into a sparrow, and she used to come and call out when Pock Face was combing her hair: 'Comb once, peep; comb twice, peep; comb thrice, up to the spine of Pock Face.' And the wicked wife answered: 'Comb once, comb twice, comb thrice, to the spine of Beauty.' The scholar was very mystified by this conversation, and he said to the sparrow: 'Why do you sing like that? Are you by any chance my wife? If you are, call three times, and I will put you in a golden cage and keep you as a pet.' The sparrow called out three times, and the scholar bought a golden cage to keep it in. The ugly sister was very angry when she saw that her husband kept the sparrow in a cage, and she secretly killed it and threw it into the garden, where it was once more transformed into a bamboo with many shoots. When Pock Face ate them, an ulcer formed on her tongue, but the scholar found them excellent. ✂ (5)

The wicked woman became suspicious again and had the bamboo cut down and made into a bed, but when she lay on it innumerable needles pricked her, while the scholar found it extremely comfortable. Again she became very cross and threw the bed away. ✂ (3)

Next door to the scholar lived an old woman who sold money-bags. One day, on her way home, she saw the bed and thought to herself: 'No one has died here, why have they thrown the bed away? I shall take it,' and she took the bed into her house and passed a very comfortable night. ✂ (4)

The next day, she saw that the food in the kitchen was ready cooked. She ate it up, but naturally she felt a little nervous, not having any idea who could have prepared it. Thus for several days she found she could have dinner the moment she came home, but finally, being no longer able to contain her anxiety, she came back early one afternoon and went into the kitchen, where she saw a dark shadow washing rice. She ran up quickly and clasped the shadow round the waist. 'Who are you?' she asked, 'and why do you cook food for me?' The shadow replied: 'I will tell you everything. I am the wife of your neighbour the scholar and am called "Beauty". My sister threw me into the well and I was drowned, but my soul was not dispersed. Please give me a rice-pot as head, a stick as hand, a dish-cloth as entrails, firehooks as feet, and then I can assume my former shape again.' The old woman gave her what she asked for, and in a moment a beautiful girl appeared, and the old woman was so delighted at seeing such a charming girl, that she questioned her very closely. She told the old woman everything, and then said: 'Old woman, I have got a bag, which you must offer for sale outside the scholar's house. If he comes out, you must sell it to him.' And she gave her an embroidered bag. ✂ (5)

The next day the old woman stood outside the scholar's house and shouted that she had a bag for sale. Maddened by the noise, he came out to ask what kind of bags she sold, and she showed him Beauty's embroidered bag. 'Where did you get this bag?' he asked. 'I gave it to my wife.' The old woman then told the whole story to the scholar, who was overjoyed to hear that his wife was still alive. He arranged everything with the old woman, laid down a red cloth on the ground, and brought Beauty back to his house.

When Pock Face saw her sister return, she gave her no peace. She began to grumble and say that the woman was only pretending to be Beauty, and that in point of fact she was a spirit. She wanted to have a trial to see which was the genuine wife. Beauty, also, would not admit herself in the wrong, and said: 'Good. We will have a test.' Pock Face suggested that they should walk on eggs, and whoever broke the shells would be the loser, but although she broke all the eggs, and Beauty none, she refused to admit her loss and insisted on another trial. This time they were to walk up a ladder made of knives. Beauty went up and down first without receiving the tiniest scratch, but before Pock Face had gone two steps her feet were cut to the bone. Although she had lost again, she insisted on another test, that of jumping into a cauldron of hot oil. She hoped that Beauty, who would have to jump in first, would be burnt. Beauty, however, was quite unharmed by the boiling oil, but the wicked sister fell into it and did not appear again.

Reading Games, © Jill Hadfield and Charles Hadfield 1995

ARIES ... Sign of the Ram (21 March – 20 April)

Their life-style

... tant state of paradox. ... They're idealistic but ... believe they're the ... deep down they doubt ... you.

Their angle

Abrupt in manner, arrogant in conduct, frank in speech, they charge their way through their day and don't even notice if they trample down a daisy or two in transit.

Their problems

The only thing which really throws them is inner conflict, and then they become nervous, timid, halting – just another sheep.

Their attitude

Typical Ram personalities have minds that go with their passion for rushing into things. With them, courage, quick decisions, bright ideas and competition are the breath of life.

Individual expertise, speed and a forceful personality are the Ram's answer to everybody's problems. Solid teamwork or plodding through statistics is strictly for others.

Action is the Ram's motivating force.

Never try to order Ram personalities around. They can't bear taking orders, uncommunicative friends, or layabouts.

TAURUS ... Sign of the Bull (21 April – 21 May)

Their life-style

Bull personalities are committed sensualists of beautiful simplicity. All they ask is a satisfying partner, a comfortable domain, and a regular supply of good, plain food. But cross them, coerce them or try to fence them in and you'll wonder what started the earthquake.

Their angle

Slightly ponderous in manner, persistent in conduct, slow of speech. No one could describe them as selfish but they can be very stubborn and detest being contradicted.

Their problems

In fact, their only problem is their capacity for sudden blind rage. Then they become violent, destructive, terrible – satisfied with nothing less than total demolition.

Their attitude

Typical Bull personalities have minds that go with the calm, comfortable, simple life in which there is always time to pause and watch the grass grow.

They'll work on solid, worthwhile projects with a tenacity of purpose that has to be seen to be believed. Construction is the Bull's motivating force.

Never try to push or hustle Bull personalities. They can't bear ugly surroundings, fair-weather friends or pushy, restless people.

GEMINI ... Sign of the Twins (22 May – 21 June)

Their life-style

Geminis actually do have twin personalities, both as different as chalk and cheese. This duality adds up to double trouble for any ordinary person trying to understand them. As a result, even their nearest and dearest find them 'two-faced'.

Their angle

Quick with their wits, alert, sympathetic and affable, they never ever lose their air of youthful let's-have-a-party type enthusiasm.

Their problems

As long as the sun's shining and gay, gregarious Twin Number One's in charge – they're everybody's friend. But let the storm clouds gather and the first flash of lightning will often reveal the self-centred, chilly, disgruntled profile of Twin Number Two.

Their attitude

Typical Twin personalities have minds that fit their insatiable urge for new places, people and ideas. Mentally and physically restless.

Short-term learning appeals and long-term study appalls. They skim over the surface of life, winning their way with their quick, double-edged wits, chatting glibly and gaily. Versatility is the Twin's motivating force.

They can't bear hung-up characters, slow minds or dreamy, illogical reasoning. Never try to restrain Twin personalities.

CANCER ... Sign of the Crab (22 June – 23 July)

Their life-style

Crab personalities live in a swirling sea of emotions, which sweep them along – ebbing and flowing, rising and falling like the tides of the ocean. But until you really know them, you'd never suspect it!

Their angle

Slightly gruff in manner, immediately sensitive to atmosphere, careful of speech, they pick their way over the rocks of life with judicious caution. Always prudent, sometimes ruthless but never reckless, they have a strong sense of duty.

Their problem

The only thing that stops them in their tracks an encounter with a stranger whose perspicacity is sharp enough to see though them.

Their attitude

Typical Crab personalities have a tough surface, concealing exceptional softness of heart. They can immerse themselves absolutely in work or play with unwavering determination. Tenacity is the Crab's motivating force.

They can't bear inquisitive strangers, capricious minds or untrustworthy people. Never neglect or rebuff Crab personalities.

LEO ... Sign of the Lion (24 July – 23 August)

Their life-style

Lordly in manner, commanding in conduct, slightly patronising in speech.
Lion personalities are benevolent despots.

Their problems

Indeed, it is this supreme faith in their own superiority and strength which is their greatest weakness. It leaves them open to persuasion by flattery and can make them behave pompously and snobbishly, which in turn leads to wrong decisions and foolish posturing.

Their attitude

Typical Lion personalities have minds which go with their high, wide and handsome life-style.
They are never mean-spirited or petty, often generous to the point of lunatic extravagance. Lion personalities love to be loved and often are – for those reasons.
Power is the Lion's motivating force.
They can't bear inhibited characters, or being dictated to. Never try to outdo Lion personalities.

VIRGO ... Sign of the Virgin (24 August – 23 September)

Their life-style

Virgin personalities are purists.

Their angle

Basically loners, they usually look for occupations where they have only to rely on their own impeccable judgement. Professions like law, medicine and journalism thus appeal.
Slightly reserved in manner, down-to-earth in conduct, quick but sparing of speech, they possess talents, great industry, keen intellect – and so rarely fail.

Their problems

Sadly, the absolute dedication of Virgin personalities don't exactly encourage close friendships or warm communication.

Their attitude

Typical Virgin personalities have minds that fit their neat, trim and immaculate appearance. Cool-hearted, clear-minded and incredibly diligent, they methodically pursue chosen objectives with quiet dedication.
Their recreations are invariably some other form of work.
They can't bear pretentious behaviour or pomposity.
Never push Virgin personalities into accepting second-best efforts or second-best relationships.

LIBRA ... Sign of the Scales (24 September – 23 October)

Their life-style

Scales personalities function with the perfect predictability of a beautiful but unsophisticated mechanical device.

Their angle

Agreeable in manner, tactful in conduct, they genuinely strive to balance the scales of life and create a calm, comfortable, civilised world.

Their problems

The only defect is their superficiality. Because they see but rarely feel, they do not understand that human responses are frequently inharmonious, often unbalanced with pride or passion.

Their attitude

Typical Scales personalities have minds that work like a perfectly tuned machine plus an elegant, appearance.
They are attracted to civilised occupations.
Harmony is the Scales motivating force.
They can't bear discourteous people or freakish attitudes.
Never be inconsistent or unjust with Scales personalities.

SCORPIO ... Sign of the Scorpion (24 October – 22 November)

Their life-style

Scorpion personalities are born to be misunderstood, loved or hated but never ignored. They act with a ruthless intensity which rarely counts the cost to themselves or to others.

Their angle

They rely on hunches and intuition. Because of their deep secret minds, Scorpion personalities work in mysterious ways.

Their problems

The only defect in their powerful and compelling personality is their refusal to trust any leadership but their own and their desire to revenge themselves on those who wrong or oppose them. They are loyal friends and are dangerous enemies.

Their attitude

Usually highly intelligent, they apply themselves with silent determination to the achievement of their private dreams. The rougher the competition, the more they thrive. For the Scorpion, winning is the name of every game. Victory is the Scorpion's motivating force.
They can't bear insincerity or stuffy, formal parties.
Never deliberately deceive Scorpion personalities or make them promises you can't keep.

Reading Games, © Jill Hadfield and Charles Hadfield 1995

SAGITTARIUS ... Sign of the Centaur
(23 November – 21 December)

Their life-style

Centaur personalities are creatures divided against themselves. Their instincts are crude, easily satisfied and unbridled. (They emanate from the horse half!) Their thoughts are noble, high-minded and pure. (They emanate from the human half!) Their actions can be dictated by either half or by both halves together.

Their angle

Tact or delicacy is beyond them. They are open in manner, confident in conduct, jovial in speech.

Their problems

The chief defect in their big, bold and breezy natures is their animal exuberance, which often leads them into empty boasting.

Their attitude

Typical Centaur personalities have minds that fit their favourite maxim: 'a healthy mind in a healthy body'. Most forms of athletic effort exert a lifelong attraction, particularly those connected with horses and dogs. In work and play, they take wins and losses with equally exuberant good humour. The race is always for the excitement – not the gold cups. Enthusiasm is the Centaur's motivating force.

They can't bear frosty manners, undemocratic people, or gloomy behaviour.

Never try to control Centaur personalities.

CAPRICORN ... Sign of the Goat
(22 December – 20 January)

Their life-style

Goat personalities are individuals with one-track minds. Their track is narrow, lonely and the signpost always says 'The Way to the Top'. For 'Tops' – professional, social and emotional – are all Goats really care about. They must climb every Everest they encounter – or die in the attempt (which in fact, sometimes happens). Desire for prestige and the financial recognition of it, drive them, onward and upward.

Their angle

Austere, taciturn, routine-minded, they leap to success until the topmost summit is theirs.

Their problems

By far the most materialistic of the twelve personality types, they may sadly illustrate the old maxim: 'The higher they fly, the harder they fall'.

Their attitude

Typical Goat personalities have minds that go with their strong, trim, wiry bodies. They're mentally and physically built of endurance, survival, agility. Learning appeals. Sports do not. Throughout their lives they never lose the same persevering approach to everything. Tradition is the Goat's motivating force.

They can't bear being talked down to, or mixing with irresponsible, frivolous people.

Never nag Goat personalities.

AQUARIUS ... Sign of the Water-Bearer
(21 January – 19 February)

Their life-style

Water-Bearer personalities are the original. They confidently expect all troubles to melt away and are positively shocked when they don't.

Nevertheless, the daily disappointments of life never give them pause and they travel cheerily on.

Their angle

Altruistic, independent and spontaneous, Water-Bearer personalities can be lost in their thoughts of brotherly love and dreaming their utopian dreams while the bus goes without them.

Their problems

People often regard them as eccentrically individualist to the point of being unreal.

Their attitude

Neither organised sport nor study have much appeal to Water-Bearers. They are always far too busy working out bigger, broader and better designs for living. Inventiveness is the Water-Bearer's motivating force.

They can't bear meanness in money or spirit.

Never preach orthodoxy or conventional standards to Water-Bearer personalities.

PISCES ... Sign of the Fish (20 February – 20 March)

Their life-style

Fish personalities are creatures of the depths, forever pulled this way and that by the conflicting forces of their physical and spiritual selves. They think deeply on all kinds of problems, but aren't really interested in solving them.

Their angle

Tentative in manner, hesitant in conduct and often vague in speech. Because of their idealism, Fish personalities are lifelong 'Love thy neighbour' types.

Their problems

The major defect is their total lack of worldliness. Because they feel the need of others with such intensity, they are too easily swept away by (often misplaced) trust only to find themselves left with nothing.

Their attitude

Idealism is the Fish's motivating force.

They can't bear intolerance. Never put a control on Fish personalities.

The Rat
personality

The Rat is adaptable and creative, not lacking in flair or inventiveness. But, quick-witted, bright and sociable, the Rat also tends towards ostentatiousness.

The Rat's outward personality is certainly appealing: but below the surface there is sometimes a crafty and opportunist character, who tends to 'use' friends before eventually losing or dropping them, for one reason or another.

In financial matters, Rat-personalities are erratic: budgeting carefully when money is scarce, but spending lavishly instead of saving in times of plenty.

In a business situation Rats make great planners.

The Ox
personality

The Ox is steadfast and methodical, reliable and sensible. Suspicious of anything that is untried and unproven, the Ox fears taking the initiative. Being so thoroughly dependable, the Ox may rise to positions of authority; but not to administrative posts where quick-thinking and a flair for making immediate decisions are essential.

The Ox may be unromantic, but there is no lack of affection for a few select friends. Preferring such company to a wide circle of acquaintances, the Ox can be both loyal and possessive.

In business, the Ox often brings prosperity – not through imagination and risk, but as a result of logical thought, resolute practicality and honest endurance. What others achieve through flair and invention is what the Ox achieves through routine and patience.

The Tiger
personality

The Tiger is a born leader, fiercely competitive, never afraid to fight. Not easily influenced, the Tiger's natural authority is seldom disputed.

The Tiger is also a great stimulant to others, through brilliant conversation, where unexpected and novel ideas are constantly paraded.

But while bravery, rashness and impetuosity are the hall-marks of the Tiger-personality, Tigers can be warm, sincere, and even ardent in love. In this and other respects, the Tiger is unlikely to be restrained by convention.

The Tiger's competitive streak is excellent material for business activities. Tigers are likely to succeed in sales, personnel management and uniformed careers. They should take care, however, that their manner does not gain them enemies along the way.

The Hare
personality

The Hare needs company, and needs to belong to an established crowd. Safely within their social circle, Hares feel protected and secure; outside it, they are reserved and withdrawn.

The typical Hare will be submissive, even humble, in a constant effort to avoid all confrontations. Happiest with friends, this kind and benevolent lover of conversation, reading and literary pursuits may appear rather meek.

Traditionally associated with clear-sightedness, the Hare is an excellent judge of character, with an instinct for recognising sincerity in others and an ability for sensing falsehood.

Hare personalities are often gifted healers.

The Dragon
personality

A lover of the exotic, the Dragon is one of the most flamboyantly extrovert characters of the Chinese astrological calendar. Always elegant Dragon-types are to the forefront of the fashion scene with a very individual sense of style. Blessed with an extraordinarily fertile imagination, the Dragon is forever dreaming up fresh schemes and ideas, few of which are wholly practical. Such a character can be the despair of friends, and at work may even cause chaos if not surrounded by people capable of picking up the fragments of abandoned projects. Strong and decisive, Dragons would become wealthy were it not for the fact that spectacular gains are often offset by the money they waste.

Dragons delight in any form of adulation, and both socially and in business they tend to seek out the bright lights. They are thus ideally suited to careers on the stage, but in general any sphere where there is close contact with the public is rewarding.

The Snake
personality

Snake personalities often make their way to the top, but they are by no means pushy, using others to get them there. They ensure that they are in the right place at the right time, which means when the right people are there as well. Snake-types are also adept at giving the impression that they know far more about a subject than they do. They are not averse to double-dealing when it suits them. Fond of scandal, they are not above creating it.

The Snake has an aptitude for research, detection or academia, all areas which should satisfy the Snake's analytical brain.

The Horse
personality

Whether male or female, Horse personalities feel more comfortable in the company of their own kind. The Horse may be afraid of the opposite sex, overawed by them, worship them, or disdain them, but relate to them – never.

Sporty and sociable, the Horse is the sort of person for whom clubs were invented. But sociability does not rule out competitiveness, although in sports the Horse prefers to be part of a team effort rather than perform as an individual. The Horse needs to feel successful, and to be seen as one of the gang.

Horse-types are good talkers, never short of conversation, though less quick with ready ideas and always keen to hear other people's opinions. Love of social contact remains the most important force in the Horse's life; and whatever career is chosen, ideally it will involve close liaison with others.

The Sheep
personality

The Sheep is associated with affection, caring, trust and selflessness.

The positive side of the Sheep-nature is best seen in its artistic talent. This usually, however, finds expression in craftsmanship rather than originality.

Complacent and avoiding confrontation whenever possible, the Sheep is ever diplomatic and often succeeds where active aggression would fail.

The Sheep is a follower rather than a leader, and thus operates best in the company of others. No Sheep, however, is happy when being directed by others, preferring a democratic community, where decisions are shared. In times of crisis, the Sheep urgently needs guidance and direction.

The Sheep may be involved, either professionally or voluntarily, in social work of some description, while a sensitivity for the arts may well lead to a career in music or a craft.

The Monkey
personality

An inventive and agile mind, together with an insatiable curiosity, produce a quick-witted schemer, sometimes unscrupulous. The Monkey is never at a loss for words, or ideas, but hides a fundamental insecurity behind a mask of impudence.

Despite apparent popularity, the Monkey is never taken seriously, and this lack of recognition often leads to frustration.

Older and wiser Monkeys are able to channel their energetic and fertile imaginations into the solving of extremely complex problems; and such skills might be used by the micro-surgeon or the counterfeiter.

Generally, the Monkey is extremely versatile and can do well at almost anything. Success, however, can easily go to the Monkey's head, bringing out arrogance which often alienates friends. But it is rarely long before the Monkey's agreeable humour and sociability win them back again.

The Rooster
personality

Abrasive and aggressive, the Rooster frequently alienates people. The Rooster is resolute in pursuing a career and has a shrewd business sense.

The Rooster is alert, with precise attention to detail. The problems arrive when so many projects are taken on that some get lost. This happens, not just in business, but in personal relationships as well, when the quieter, more reserved members of the Rooster's social circle or family may be neglected or forgotten.

Stamina in business and vitality in play contribute to making the Rooster a stimulating companion. The Rooster has high ideals and, being a perfectionist, has little tolerance for people whose standards are second-rate.

The Dog
personality

Fidelity, honesty and humour are among the traits of a typical Dog-character. Such a likeable personality easily makes friends and, being a steady worker, the Dog becomes a trusted and valued member of any community.

The Dog, however, is handicapped by conservatism, and takes a long time to adjust to major changes. Nothing is really ever as good as it was 'in the old days'.

Intensely defensive where friends and family are concerned, the Dog will not stand by while others are maligned. The Dog has a sympathetic ear for other people's troubles and is always ready with a shoulder to cry on. Rare displays of violent anger are almost always justified; but wrongs are quickly forgotten.

Very active and liking sports of all kinds, the Dog can always be relied on to join in at social events, especially if these are outdoors. This can, however, lead to friction at home unless the partner is particularly understanding of the Dog's eagerness to mix.

The Pig
personality

The Pig's ambitions are concerned not so much with career, but the benefits which come at the end of it. The Pig looks forward to retirement. Pigs are home-lovers whose prime concern is the family. They are particularly natural beings, shunning displays or pretence, and enjoying company and jollity generally. Caring and industrious, Pigs are far from lazy; their homes bear evidence of an aptitude for carpentry, needlework, and other domestic skills.

In business, too, Pigs are the finisher, the ones who put the last necessary touches to a project, and in this respect they may become extremely successful financially. But they are naive and trusting, falling easy prey to the confidence trickster. Pig personalities enjoy such caring professions as nursing or counselling. Locally, the Pig will almost certainly be known as a good neighbour.

Hard-working, hospitable and trusting, the Pig gets on well with most people, generally possessing a large and varied collection of friends.

Make notes on your star sign or year animal under the headings.

Positive characteristics

Negative characteristics

Habits

Problems

Way of life or typical career

How they behave towards others

How others should behave towards them

A Dream almanac

ABROAD – To dream of being abroad, in a foreign country, denotes a change in your situation in life; you are likely to be unsettled in life, and to change your locality.

ACORNS – When you dream of acorns, it is a good sign; it betokens health, strength, and worldly abundance; if single, you are likely to marry well, and have a numerous family. To a married woman it denotes the birth of twins. To business men it is the omen of prosperity and wealth; and to all it is a good sign. To those in love it denotes success and happiness. To those in difficulties, a speedy recovery.

ALLIGATOR – This denotes a sly, crafty enemy; and such a dream should excite caution.

ALMONDS – To dream of eating sweet almonds indicates future enjoyment, probably by travel in a distant country. If you relish the almonds, every undertaking will be prosperous; if the taste is bitter, your enterprise will fail; and the expenses of it will be costly.

APPLES – This is a very good dream; it indicates a long and happy life, success in business and in love. For a woman with child to dream of apples denotes that she will have a son who will be very great and wealthy. A good dream for speculation.

ARROW – To dream that an arrow is shot at you, and that it penetrates your body, is a bad omen. Some person or persons are scheming against you.

BATS – To dream of seeing a bat flying in the air signifies that you have an enemy. If it appears flying by daylight you need not fear, but if by night, you are in danger. For a young person in love to dream of a bat denotes that you will have a dangerous rival to annoy you.

BEAR – To dream of seeing a bear, expect trouble, and that some enemy will injure you; and that if you travel, you will meet with hardships, but the end of your journey will be safely accomplished, and the object achieved. To dream that you are fighting with a bear, and kill it, is a favourable sign of your overcoming a foe.

BEAUTY – To dream that you are beautiful, is a dream of contradiction denoting that sickness may debilitate your strength. To dream of any friend as beautiful, denotes their sickness.

BED – To dream of being in bed signifies a very early marriage; and to dream of making a bed indicates a change of residence, and that you will live away from home a long time. To dream of sitting upon a young girl's bedside is certainly a sign of marriage.

BEEF – To dream of eating beef indicates that you will always live in plenty, though you may not be rich; but to dream of beef, and that you have not the power to eat, denotes that you will be dependent on another's bounty.

BELLS – To dream of hearing the bells ring is a fortunate sign. It is a sign of coming good news. To the young it foretells a happy and early marriage to the person so ardently loved by them. To persons in business it denotes the acquirement of a fortune. It foretells advancement in your trade or profession.

BOAT – If you dream that you are sailing in a boat or ship and the water is smooth and the weather pleasant, it is a lucky omen, denoting a prosperous business, and happiness in marriage. If the water is rough and muddy you will have to labour all your life. If you fall into the water you must beware of disaster.

BOX – If you dream that you are opening a box, and looking for something in it, and cannot find it, it is an indication that you are going to be troubled about money matters; or that you will suffer some pecuniary loss.

BOX – To dream of the plant 'Box', implies long life and prosperity, with a happy marriage and large family.

BRACELET – To dream that you are wearing a bracelet, you will shortly be married to a wealthy person. If you dream that you find a bracelet it is a sign of a coming fortune; if you dream that someone put upon your hand a bracelet you will soon fall in love, and be accepted, or if already in love, you will be married without delay.

Dream

I dreamt that I was trying to climb a steep hill. The hill was covered in brambles and I kept getting caught in the brambles and scratched by the thorns. I began to cry because I thought I would never get out and reach the top of the hill. Suddenly I found that I was flying in the air over the brambles and up into the sky over the top of the hill. The sun was shining and I felt very light and suddenly very happy. I landed on the other side of the hill in a huge orchard full of many different trees: apples almonds and lemons. The trees had many branches and were laden with fruit. There was a ladder reaching up into one of the trees. I climbed up the ladder into the tree and found I was surrounded by ripe yellow lemons, shining in the sunlight. I began to pick and eat the lemons – somehow I was sure they would taste sweet and so they did!

B Dream almanac

BRAMBLES – To dream of briars and brambles and that you are injured by them, is a very unlucky dream; it denotes difficulties and problems to be overcome all your life. If you are not hurt by them, you will have trouble, but of a short duration.

BRANCH – If you dream that you see a tree full of branches, it denotes abundance, and a numerous family – a happy posterity.

BREAD – to dream of seeing a quantity of bread is a sign of sufficiency of worldly possessions. If you dream of eating good bread, you will enjoy good health, and live long; but if the bread is burned it is a bad sign. To dream of baking bread is also bad, generally denoting affliction and sorrow.

BRIDE, BRIDESMAID, OR BRIDEGROOM - This is a dream of contradiction. To dream that you take any of these characters is very unlucky, it is a sure forerunner of grief and disappointment.

BRIDGE – To dream that you are crossing a bridge in the daytime, foretells a change of situation. If any person interrupts you, it implies that the one you love will deceive you; but if you pass along without any impediment, you will succeed in your undertakings, and prosper. If you dream that you are walking towards a bridge that is broken down, do not make any hasty change in your situation for you will not be successful.

CAMELS – To dream of these wonderfully hard and patient creatures, denotes that you will have heavy burdens to bear, and disasters to meet, all of which, however, you will bear with heroism; but the time will come when you will be entirely rid of them, and become very happy.

CANDLES – To dream that you are making candles, denotes that you will be very useful to others; if you dream that you are buying candles, it indicates feasting and rejoicing. To dream that you see a candle burning brightly, portends that you will receive a letter containing pleasing intelligence; but if you dream that you see a candle snuffed or blown out, it denotes the death of a friend.

CATTLE – If you dream of cattle grazing in a pasture, it is a good sign of prosperity and affluence. If you dream of driving cattle it portends that if you are diligent and industrious, you will make money. Black and large-horned cattle denote many violent enemies.

CATHEDRAL – To dream that you are in a cathedral denotes that you will have enough money to enable you to travel and see the sights of the world. To married persons, it denotes good children, some of whom will be eminent in the church.

CLOCK - To dream you hear the clock strike denotes a speedy marriage, and that you will be very comfortable in life. To dream that you are counting the hours, if in the forenoon, it indicates much happiness; but if in the afternoon, some misfortune and danger. If the clock strikes roughly, and not the full hours, it denotes an upset in your health.

CLOUDS – To dream of dark clouds suspended over you, indicates that you will have to pass through great sorrows. But if the clouds break, and roll away, your sorrows will pass away, and prosperity will follow.

CORNFIELD – To dream of cornfields, or corn, is a most favourable omen. It betokens health, a happy family, a prosperous trade, great wealth. Speculations will prosper. Love-life will be a perennial honeymoon.

DARK – If you dream that you are in darkness and cannot find your way, and you stumble, it denotes a change in your temporal affairs for the worse; by your imprudence, you will dreadfully commit yourself. But if you dream that you emerge from the darkness, and behold the sun, it denotes your ultimate escape; you will be happy, and regain your reputation.

DANCE – This is a favourable dream; it indicates that you will be the recipient of great favour and honour; that your plans will succeed; that in love you will win the hand of the person you desire.

Dream 2

I dreamt that I was alone in the desert. It was evening and as it began to grow dark a cloud of bats appeared and began to attack me. I was terrified and crouched down with my hands over my head to protect myself, but their beaks were very sharp. Suddenly, although it was night, the sun came out and immediately the bats flew away. Now that the sun was shining I could see that there was a river not far away, and tied to the bank was a small boat. I thought at first it was a mirage, but as I walked towards it I found it was real. I got in the boat and floated down the river. The water was as smooth as glass and gradually the desert gave way to orchards on either side. The river got wider and wider and soon flowed into the ocean where I was gently rocked on the waves. The boat seemed to guide itself across the sea and eventually we came to a small fertile island with brilliant green trees and bright flowers. I got out onto the beach and began to walk inland and suddenly found myself in a dense forest where the trees were full of bright red and green parrots.

Reading Games, © Jill Hadfield and Charles Hadfield 1995

C Dream almanac

DESERT – To dream that you are travelling across a desert, is a sign of a difficult journey, especially if you dream that the weather is wet and boisterous. If you see the sun shine, your journey, and all affairs, will be safe and prosperous.

DRINK – To dream that you are drinking at a fountain, is a sign of much happiness and enjoyment. If the water is muddy, it denotes approaching trouble. If you are thirsty, and cannot find water, it portends that your trials will have to be borne without any assistance.

ECHO – To dream you hear an echo to your own voice denotes that the letter you have sent will be met by a favourable answer, that the person to whom you have proposed will accept you; that your children will be beautiful, and good. Mind you do not idolise these little echoes! You will also hear of an absent friend.

EGGS – To dream of seeing a great number of eggs, indicates success in trade and in love. It also denotes a happy marriage and good children, and great prosperity. If you hope for advancement to a better job, or position, it shall be yours. To dream that the eggs prove rotten denotes unfaithful and treacherous friends and lovers. To dream of eating eggs portends great enjoyment.

FACES – If you dream that you see your own face in a glass, it is a sign that your secret plans will be discovered. If you see in dreaming many strange faces, it portends a change of your present abode, and associations. If you gaze in your dream upon the faces of friends, etc., it is a sign of a party, or wedding, to which you will be invited.

FACTORY – To dream that you are inspecting a factory, when all is in operation, denotes that your trade will flourish, by which you will acquire much wealth, and be very useful all your life. It also betokens a time of commercial prosperity generally.

FAILURE – This is a dream of contradiction. To dream that you fail in business – that you fail in securing the person you love – that your plans do not succeed, indicates that, by wise and cautious procedure, in all things you will succeed.

FAIR – It is very unlucky to dream of being at a fair, it portends negligence in your business, and also false friends. The persons about you are not so honest as they should be. Through rivalry the lover is likely to suffer loss.

FAIRY – To dream that you see a fairy, is a very favourable dream. Poor men have had this dream, and afterwards become very rich. Engagement and happy marriage will follow this dream by either sex. Indicates rapid rise for a man in his business or profession.

FALCON – This is a very bad dream. There is a foe near you, full of envy, injuring you with the tongue, and mind he or she does not injure you with the hands.

FALL – To dream that you fall from an eminence, from a tree, or the edge of a precipice, denotes a loss of situation, and of property. If you are in love, you bestow your attachments in vain; you will never marry the person. To the tradesman, it denotes a failing business, embarrassment, etc.

FALSE – An unusual dream. It indicates the very reverse, true, firm, and lasting friendships; a lover not of mushroom growth, but like an evergreen, always perennial!

FAMINE – This is a dream of contradiction, denoting national prosperity, and individual comfort, in wealth and much enjoyment. You will have many friends, a true lover, and a happy family.

FARM – To dream that you are taking a farm, denotes advancement. Probably someone will bequeath property to you, and make you independent. If you dream of visiting a farm, and of partaking of its produce, it is a sign of good health. If you are single and unengaged, and a young person there serves you with something to eat and drink, you will soon be very agreeably in love.

Dream 3

I was in a huge stone cathedral, feeling very cold. There was music at the far end and as I walked towards it I suddenly found that I was no longer in the cathedral but flying over it on a large bird. I looked down below me and saw the cathedral towers and all around the cathedral square was a big, bustling market where people were selling eggs, bread, and all kind of fruit and vegetables. As I flew over the cathedral the bells began to ring and the clock struck twelve. I was so surprised that I fell from the bird but landed on the back of a white horse that was galloping out of the town. Soon we had left the town and were out in the open country.

We rode through a cornfield and then the horse jumped over a fence into a big green field where a lot of rabbits were playing happily in the sunshine.

D Dream almanac

FAT – To dream of getting fat is an indication of illness and also of lovers' quarrels.

FATHER – To dream of your father, denotes that he loves you; if he be dead, it is sign of affliction.

FAWN – For a young man or young woman to dream of a young deer, is a sign of inconstancy. If a married woman has such a dream, it portends fruitfulness.

FEVER – To dream you have a fever denotes constant change in your business circumstances. They will alternate: sometimes you will be prosperous sometimes poor.

FLOWERS – To dream that you are gathering beautiful and fragrant flowers, it is an indication of prosperity; you will be very fortunate in all you undertake. If in your dream, you bind the flowers into a bouquet, it portends your very agreeable marriage. If the bouquet gets loose, and the flowers appear to be scattered, your brightest prospects, and most sanguine hopes will be blasted.

FLYING – To dream of flying denotes that you will escape many difficulties and dangers. It denotes success in trade and in love. Very likely you will have to travel. If you dream that you are trying to fly very high, it is an indication that you will aspire after a position which you will never reach, and for a job for which you are not qualified.

FOG – It denotes great uncertainty. You wish to be accepted as a lover. It is doubtful. You have applied to your friends for assistance. They will never give it. You are speculating in shares, they may ruin you. The dream is unfavourable. If you dream that the fog clears away and the sun shines, your state will be happily reversed – uncertainty will vanish.

HILLS – To dream of ascending a high steep hill and you are unable to arrive at the top, it is a sign that you will have to labour and toil all your life, and have many difficulties and troubles to overcome. It denotes that those in love will not find their path easy.

HONEY – To dream you are eating honey denotes good health, long life, prosperity and great enjoyment. Your business will be all you can wish, lucrative, raising you to independence. It denotes that your lover is virtuous, sincere, and very fond of you. It would be death to part from you. It denotes that the husband, or the wife, will be of a sweet disposition, industrious, affectionate and faithful.

HORSE – Dreaming of this noble animal is generally good. To dream that you are riding a handsome and good horse betokens future independence and happiness. But if it throws you, it denotes that your purposes will be thwarted. If you dream that horsemen approach you, it foretells that you will receive news from a distant friend. To dream of white horses, denotes a marriage, yours, if you are riding upon it.

ISLAND – To dream that you are on a desolate island implies the loss of your lover. If it appears a fertile island, covered with vegetation, it implies that your present lover will prove unfaithful; but you will soon meet with a more favourable match.

JEWELS – It is always a good dream, the harbinger of great prosperity, and a great amount of wealth. To dream that the one you love gives you jewels is a sign that his affection is real, and that he will certainly marry you. If a young man dreams that he sees his loved one adorned with jewels, it foretells his speedy and happy union; that his bride will possess a sweet and lovely disposition. To dream that both you and your lover are counting and inspecting jewels, denotes numerous healthy, and fortunate offspring.

KEY – To dream that you lose a key, denotes disappointment and displeasure. To dream you give a key denotes a marriage; to find or receive one, the birth of a child; to dream of many keys, denotes riches, as the result of a flourishing business.

LADDER – This dream has great import. You will reach the top of the ladder of the ambition to which you aspire. If in business you will prosper. It is the portent of wealth, honour and glory. Scholars and students will reach the climax of their ambition.

Dream 4

I dreamt that I was reading a newspaper by the light of a brightly burning candle. The article I was reading was about a leopard that had escaped from the zoo. Suddenly I wasn't in the house any more, but riding on the back of the leopard as it ran away from the zoo. The leopard carried me deep into the mountains where it began to snow heavily. Then the leopard disappeared and I was alone in the mountains in the snowstorm. I knew that if I could find my way to the top of the mountains I would be able to see where to go, so I tried to struggle uphill, but the snow made it difficult to walk. Suddenly from behind an enormous rock there appeared a big brown bear, growling and snarling and coming towards me. I turned to run but it was too late. The bear attacked me and we began to fight. I was badly wounded and bleeding but just as I had given up hope the snow stopped, the clouds began to clear and as the sun came out the bear ran off. I found that I had stopped bleeding and my wounds had disappeared. I scrambled to my feet and looked around. Somehow I had got to the top of the mountain and stretching across the valley was a rainbow.

Reading Games, © Jill Hadfield and Charles Hadfield 1995

E   Dream almanac

LEMONS – To dream you see lemons growing on a tree denotes that you will visit a foreign land, and probably marry a native of it. To dream that you eat lemons denotes you will be attacked by a dangerous illness, from which you will recover. To dream you see a great number of lemons denotes that your marriage, though pleasant for a while, will not live up to your expectations.

LEOPARD – To dream of these beautiful, yet savage creatures, indicates travel to a foreign land, where you will have to encounter many dangers and difficulties. But you will eventually overcome them, marry well, and be very prosperous and happy. It is likely that you will stay there all your life.

LETTER – Dreaming of receiving a letter sometimes indicates presents, or at least the reception of unexpected news, from a person you have not heard of for many years. To dream that you send a letter, denotes that you will soon be able to perform a generous action.

MELONS – A young man, or a young woman, who dreams of melons is destined to marry or be married to a rich foreigner, and to live in a foreign land. Such a union will be crowned with great happiness, be attended with great wealth; their children will be few, but they will be virtuous and happy.

MILK – To dream that you drink milk, foretells joy. To dream of selling milk, denotes bad trade, and disappointments in love. To dream that you give milk, denotes prosperity, and a happy marriage. To dream that you see it flowing from a woman's breast, denotes marriage, and a very large family. To dream of milking a cow, foretells abundance to the farmer, healthy cattle, and good crops.

MOUNTAIN – To dream that you are ascending a steep and rugged mountain, shows a life of toil and effort; all your endeavours to better yourself will be made difficult by unforeseen events.

NEWSPAPER – Dreaming that you are reading a newspaper shows that you will hear good news, from a distant friend, which will cause you to quit your present employment, but you will benefit from the change. You will be able to commence business on your own account, in which you will have great success. If you are a single man, it portends that you will marry a widow. To persons in love it shows that the object of their affections will travel to a distant part of the world, and it will be many years before they are again united, but their reunion will be a very happy one. To the politician, it betokens great and stirring events in the nation. To the farmer it shows a favourable season.

OCEAN – To dream that you gaze upon the ocean when it is calm, is good; when it is stormy and turbid, it augurs ill. To dream of sailing on the ocean when it is smooth, and the weather calm, with favourable breezes, certainly denotes the accomplishment of a purpose, and any object devoutly wished for, obtained. After such a dream happiness and satisfaction will follow. It prognosticates success in love affairs. To lovers, it foreshows that they will have a delicious courtship, and sail straight on into the harbour of matrimony. Your wishes will meet in one another, and you will have mutual and endearing affection.

ORCHARD – To dream that you are in an orchard, gathering fruit, agreable to the taste, as well as pleasant to the eye, foretells good fortune: you will become rich. If the fruit appears ripe, your advancement will be immediate; if green, it is yet in the distance; but it will come.

PARROTS – To dream you hear a parrot talk, foretells that you will have a very talkative person for your companion. To dream that you see many parrots foretells that you will emigrate to a foreign country, where you will settle and marry, and be very happy. You will cultivate land and by it amass wealth, and secure some honour. You will only have two children, a boy and a girl; the latter will be married to a rich man; and the former will hold an official position and be held in high esteem.

RABBITS – To dream that you see rabbits implies that you will soon have to reside in a large and populous city, where you will marry and have a very numerous family. It also foretells that you will have a flourishing business, that your plans will be successful, and that you will triumph over your enemies. For a married woman to dream of rabbits, indicates increase of family.

RAINBOW – This is a token for good. It portends change, but a change for the better.

RIVER – To dream that you see a broad, rapid, and muddy river denotes troubles and difficulties in love and business; but if the river appears calm, with a glassy surface, it foretells great happiness in love, happy marriage, beautiful children, and commercial prosperity.

SNOW – To dream that you see the ground covered with snow is a sign of prosperity, and that you will maintain an unblemished character in spite of the attempts of your enemies to blacken it. To dream that you are walking upon snow with the girl you love, foretells that she will be very beautiful. To dream that you are in a snow-storm and very much harassed, is a good dream. You will have difficulties, but you will overcome them, and come out unscathed.

Dream 5

I dreamt that I was being chased by a huge alligator. Its jaws kept opening wide to snap at me but somehow I always eluded it at the last minute. Suddenly a thick fog came down. I ran on into it. It seemed that I had lost the alligator, but now I was lost myself. I stumbled around blindly in the fog for a while, then tripped and fell, losing consciousness. When I came to, the fog had cleared and the sun had come out. I got to my feet and looked around. I was standing in the middle of a field of melons. At the edge of the field was a small house. I walked over to it and tried the door but it was locked. Feeling thirsty I picked a melon and cut it open with my knife. Inside was a bunch of keys. I tried them all, and the last one of all fitted the lock. I opened the door and stood back in amazement. The whole house was full of fruit: melons, apples, lemons and almonds, which all came tumbling out of the door as it swung open.

A The Politically Correct Dictionary

person with an alternative body image	*dog living in USA*
alternative dentation	*deaf*
aurally inconvenienced	*old*
canine American	*drunk*
career change opportunity	*fat*
cerebrally challenged	*false teeth*
charm-free	*stupid*
chemically inconvenienced	*boring*
chronologically challenged	*redundancy*

B The Politically Correct Dictionary

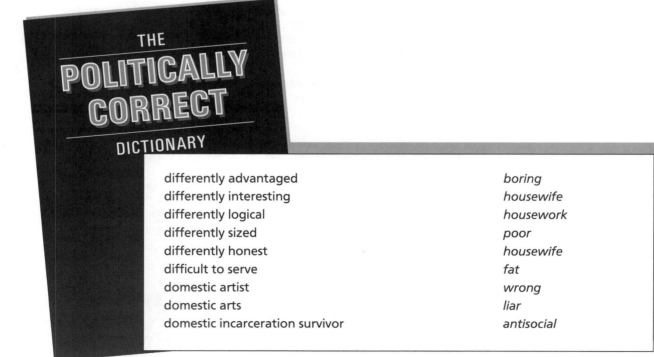

differently advantaged	*boring*
differently interesting	*housewife*
differently logical	*housework*
differently sized	*poor*
differently honest	*housewife*
difficult to serve	*fat*
domestic artist	*wrong*
domestic arts	*liar*
domestic incarceration survivor	*antisocial*

C   **The Politically Correct Dictionary**

early stages of finalization, in the	*crazy*
emotionally different	*dishonest*
ethically disorientated	*fat*
experientially enhanced	*bald*
follicularly challenged	*unfinished*
hair disadvantaged	*old*
horizontally challenged	*bald*

D   **The Politically Correct Dictionary**

in an orderly transition between career changes	*worst*
incomplete success, an	*homeless*
indefinitely idled	*mistake*
individual with temporarily unmet objectives	*unemployed*
inoperative statement	*unemployed*
involuntarily leisured	*failure*
involuntarily undomiciled	*failure*
least best	*unemployed*

E The Politically Correct Dictionary

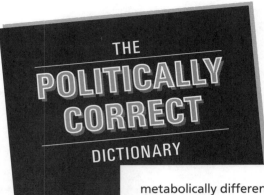

metabolically different	*evil*
morally different	*shoplifter*
motivationally deficient	*blind*
negative patient care outcome	*lazy*
non-living person	*spendthrift*
negative saver	*dead*
non-traditional shopper	*death*
optically inconvenienced	*corpse*

F The Politically Correct Dictionary

person of differing sobriety	*late*
period of economic adjustment	*addiction*
person with difficult to meet needs	*dead*
pharmalogical preference	*drunk*
reduced state of awareness, in a	*dead*
temporally challenged	*short*
terminally inconvenienced	*drunk*
underhoused	*homeless*
vertically challenged	*late*

Look at the cartoons. Write the appropriate translation in 'correct' language for the speech bubbles.

1 ....

2 ....

3 ....

4 ....

5 ....

6 ....

Index